STANDARDIZING SSADM:
METHODS, STANDARDS AND MATURITY

THE McGRAW-HILL
INTERNATIONAL SERIES IN SOFTWARE ENGINEERING

Consulting Editor

Professor D. Ince
The Open University

Titles in this Series

Further titles in this Series are listed at the back of the book

STANDARDIZING SSADM: METHODS, STANDARDS AND MATURITY

Tony Bryant

McGRAW-HILL BOOK COMPANY

London · New York · St. Louis · San Francisco · Auckland
Bogotá· Caracas · Lisbon · Madrid · Mexico · Milan
Montreal · New Delhi · Panama · Paris · San Juan · São Paulo
Singapore · Sydney · Tokyo · Toronto

Published by
McGraw-Hill Book Company Europe
Shoppenhangers Road, Maidenhead, Berkshire, SL6 2QL
Telephone 01628 23432
Fax 01628 35895

British Library Cataloguing in Publication Data
Bryant, Tony
   Standardizing SSADM:Methods, Standards
and Maturity. – (McGraw-Hill
International Software Engineering
Series)
   I. Title   II. Series
004.210218

   ISBN 0–07–709115–9

Library of Congress Cataloging-in-Publication Data
Bryant, Tony
   Methods, standards, and maturity : developing the standard for
SSADM / Tony Bryant.
      p.   cm. – (McGraw-Hill international series in software
engineering)
   Includes index.
   ISBN 0–07–709115–9
   1. Software engineering–Standards.   2. Electronic data
processing–Structured techniques.   I. Title.   II. Series.
QA76.758.B79   1995
005.1'0218–dc20   95–1440
                                                                CIP

12345 BL 98765

Typeset and illustrated by TecSet Limited, Wallington, Surrey
Printed and bound in Great Britain by Biddles Ltd, Guildford, Surrey
Printed on permanent paper in compliance with ISO standard 9706

This book is dedicated to the memory of my father
Paul Bryant (Pavel Blumenzweig)
a person of authentic standards and profound maturity

CONTENTS

PREFACE

In 1990 I was foolhardy enough to volunteer to be the SSADM Users Group representative on the newly formed BSI panel developing the standard for SSADM. This was meant to be one of those alluringly short and uncomplicated projects, requiring a minimum of input from myself, but offering considerable returns in terms of learning more about standards, making contacts with standards makers and developers, and acquiring early details of SSADM version 4.

Like all such lures, the reality proved more complex. The development of the standard was far from simple, and since it was the first time that such a standard had been developed, there were no experts or sources of wisdom: we all became experts overnight. We also had plenty of opportunity to learn from our mistakes.

Eventually, some four years later, a standard did emerge. By then the composition of the panel had altered considerably from its inception, and the standard itself had gone through several transformations. In addition I had gone from interested observer to panel convenor and standards developer, having written much of the amended text.

At the time of writing (July 1994), the standard has only been available for six weeks, so it is too soon to decide if it will be fit for purpose and of any general use. On the other hand, the lessons learned during its development can already be defined and assessed, and the salient points of the experience made available for others. That is one of the key objectives of this book.

The following chapters are meant to be of interest both to those in the standards world and those in the information systems methods world, particularly SSADM. SSADM has a large and informed body of users. These users are constantly looking for ways in which the tensions between being able to develop systems along predictable paths can be reconciled with harnessing people's innovation and experience, and changes in technology and expertise. There is no simple solution to this, but the idea of a standard was meant to provide a baseline for some aspects of development, while not precluding innovation and skill development.

During its development, the rationale for having the standard in place altered considerably. What was first seen as a legal rationale eventually, through changes in circumstances, became a less focused but still potent motivation. On the other hand, by 1994 the concept of a standard for a method had achieved considerable currency. The International Standards Organization (ISO) is currently considering such standards as part of its Software Engineering standards programme; the European Union is continuing the development of Euromethod; and several private consortia have established seminars to discuss how they might develop or contribute to such standards.

Observing some of these discussions from afar, and others from very close quarters, I have become convinced that many of the lessons learned from the SSADM experience had relevance to these initiatives. Moreover, many of the mistakes and errors that we experienced arose from misconceptions regarding the nature and purpose of standards themselves: and these same problems are already evident in these later initiatives.

I suspect that one benefit of the standards-making process is the experience it gives those involved, but that should not preclude the attempt to assist others by pointing out the likely pitfalls in the hope that if they do not avoid them, they will at least recognize them when they arise. Some of the obstacles encountered in the development of the SSADM standard will certainly be of interest to those involved in the Euromethod project, and in any standards for methods projects in information systems. They may well be relevant in the general realm of information systems standards, and in the standards world in general—although I would not wish to claim that my limited experience was sufficient basis for general pronouncements. On the contrary, one of the other aims of my argument is to counter any simplistic idea that standards are all the same, and equally applicable: hence the introduction of the discussion on maturity.

The idea of applying the concept of maturity to organizations dates back to those in the nineteenth century who introduced biological analogies into consideration of social and political entities. In recent times it has emerged more in terms of the idea of organizations having to learn and adapt to external pressures, particularly those emanating from technological change and innovation. All of this emphasizes that organizations cannot simply purchase the technology; they must prepare themselves to be able to make use of it, and monitor its effects on their general activities and culture. The continuing discussion on technology transfer is an indication of these issues. The present and growing realization that standards are important in the field of information systems has to be tempered by the understanding that not all organizations, or subdivisions within an organization, will be ready for the same levels of standardization.

ACKNOWLEDGEMENTS

This book could not have been written without the support and example offered by my wife Griselda Pollock.

I gained a great deal of experience and knowledge during my involvement with the various BSI committees and panels, and without singling anyone out in particular, I would like to thank all those who, wittingly or unwittingly, contributed to my work and maturation since 1990. Unlike the standard itself, however, what follows is my sole responsibility.

INTRODUCTION

Like the poor, standards are always with us.
Cargill (1989)

Without standards each management environment would be unique.
Marciniak and Reifer (1990)

People's conceptions of standards range from informal, intrinsic codes of behaviour and interaction to formal, sometimes obligatory stipulations dealing with products or services. Thus people talk about standards of group or individual behaviour, or of appearance and dress, at one end of the range, and about standards of building, design, and safety at the other. What the whole spectrum of understanding has in common, however, is the implication of predictability and expectation. Standards might not always be simple to define or encapsulate; but when people's assumptions are violated the 'standards' that have been transgressed become more stark. Standards bring order and security, if they are respected and observed.

In an increasing variety of professional areas of activity and influence, and other specialisms, standards in the more formal sense are becoming more visible and relevant to people's activities and expectations. The levels and intensities at which people interact, and the demands to integrate and manage disparate practices and technologies necessitate a desire for control and expectation—and standards are one route to accomplish this.

This is not to say that standards are restricted to the rarefied realms of the expert and the professional. Familiarity with and reliance on standards increasingly involves not only skilled practitioners, but also customer representatives, and suppliers of associated goods and services. Whereas previously standards were related to passively, they are now becoming seen as a key component, amenable to influence and change, in market-driven and customer—supplier exchanges.

People or organizations are no longer wholly disposed to adopt the role of consumers, complacent in their assumption that the products or services they are buying are regulated by some other, remote group of experts who define and impose standards designed to ensure some minimum degree of conformance with and performance to expectation. Instead there is an unfolding awareness that control and regulation is better achieved by active contributions from directly interested parties.

This is particularly applicable in the overall realm of information systems (IS), encompassing not only the tangible component technology information technology (IT), but also including the highly critical—but less tangible—aspects that contribute to the procurement, planning, design, development, and operation of the system itself. In fact there are relatively few standards in many key aspects of this domain, while for other aspects there is a profusion of competing or differing standards. There may be some technical control of component specifications and performance with respect to the communications and computer technology; but in many instances these go no further than some minimum view of application or compatibility. In other areas there may well not be even this minimal form of relevant standard. This is entirely understandable, since the prime concern in many of these newly emerging areas is focused on activities and procedures, which are a difficult target for control and regulation.

This is further complicated, since there is considerable conceptual confusion surrounding several key terms within this domain, such as IT, IS, and so on. (Figure I.1 offers a view of the relationships between some of these terms.)

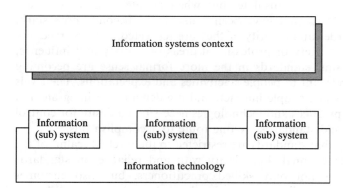

Figure I.1 Information systems and information technology in the IS context.

Essentially I shall use the term IS as follows:

An information system is a system whose objective and functions encompass the gathering, accepting, processing, storing, retrieving, producing, and presenting of information—i.e. an assortment of artefacts, services, procedures, and other adhesions.

IT can then be defined as:

The technological components of an information system, which contribute to the (effective) functioning of that system.

It might even be argued that IT should be expanded to information and communication technology (ICT), so that the communications aspect is explicitly included. This appears unnecessarily clumsy, and many definitions of IT refer to something akin to the 'microelectronics-based combination of computing and telecommunications' (Longley, 1985), or IT 'draws on the technologies of computing, electronics, telecommunications, office equipment and control engineering' (IT and Public Policy, quoted in Boaden and Lockett, 1991).

This results in a view of IS that encompasses IT, which in turn involves the basic electronics and communication components. There is then a gradation of tangibility, from the hardware components to the less definite features of the functioning IS. Component specifications are relatively easy to detail, and hence standardize and certify through conformance testing. This is particularly true for key aspects such as interfaces to or compatibility with other components. The application of this standards strategy of specification and testing is more complicated—and perhaps misguided— with respect to the less determinate products, procedures, and practices of software and information systems. This is, in part, why the effort to standardize in the IS realm is intricate—as will be explained in the later chapters (see Fig. I.2).

This highly complex situation is further exacerbated by the speed with which the technology is advancing—or at least changing—and the expanding influence IS is having. There is a need for the imposition of some level of certainty and repeatability in IS development and operation, otherwise every project and every context would be unique and there will be little chance to gain from experience and transfer of skills and resources.

In a changing context, there is increased opportunity but also increased uncertainty and risk.

Standards offer some basis for building on the former, and remedying the latter. In addition, standards offer one crucial mechanism to cultivate a situation of repeatability and expectation.

It is, therefore, not surprising that there is now a call for relevant and imposable standards across the entire IS domain. These are required to encompass not only the hardware, communications, software, and information systems themselves; but also the processes in the development

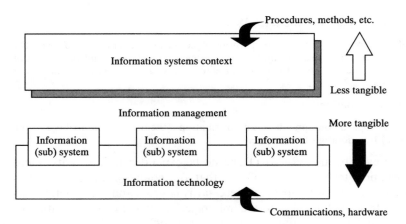

Figure I.2 Tangibility across the IT/IS spectrum.

of those systems—in particular standards for software engineering (SE) and latterly information systems engineering (ISE).

Those involved with software and systems development know that each project is unique; but standards for the processes of procurement, development, and operation are an attempt to add a layer of replication and hence a firmer basis for management and planning. This demand for standards emanates from all sides, not only from those one would expect— large-scale purchasers and consumers of IS products and services—but also from suppliers and practitioners anxious to ensure some measure of uniformity, harmony, and predictability as a context for their services, products, activities, plans, and projections.

Recognizing the potential importance of standards is one thing, getting the standards developed and disseminated is quite another. The problem is that immediately the issue of standards is raised a whole list of questions arises:

- What exactly are standards?
- How are they devised and defined?
- Who controls their application and extent?

This book seeks to answer some of these questions, explaining some general issues in the development of IS standards. The first chapter deals with the basic questions, such as the three mentioned above. Subsequent chapters expand the context within which standards can be understood, specifically from the standpoint of the IS domain, and will also explain, through an actual example, how standards can be developed in the IS realm.

The development of the SSADM standard is an interesting and instructive case study since it illustrates what can go wrong with standards development, as well as what can go right. It also forces complex IS issues into the forefront of the debate about the necessity for and efficacy of standards; and the preparedness of organizations seeking to benefit from application and enforcement of standards.

This is not to claim that what follows can be treated as some definitive statement for makers or users of standards; but it should at least clarify some issues and offer some recommendations for what to do, and what not to do in this field.

1   WHAT ARE STANDARDS? WHY STANDARDIZE?

In this chapter formal, *de jure* standards are defined, and the definition is then used to examine the relevance of standards. This then leads to a discussion of the process of standardization and some aspects of the motivations leading to standards development. Many of the problems in the development, adoption, and operation of standards seem to arise from profound misconceptions concerning the nature of standards themselves, and the processes involved in their formation. This chapter introduces some of the basic terminology, and seeks to explain the key concepts through a discussion of the BSI document *BSO: A Standard for Standards*. The chapter ends with an illustration of some of the critical aspects discussed, using the IBM PC as an example.

2   STANDARDS AND STANDARDIZATION IN THE IS/ISE DOMAIN

The first chapter offers a general outline of standards issues; this chapter extends and applies the concepts specifically to information systems and software engineering. In these computer-related areas there is much justified scepticism regarding standards. On the other hand, there is a growing demand for mechanisms to ensure and enhance predictability, control, and compatibility.

This paradox is explained with reference to the work of two authors who have each examined standards from a pragmatic and market-based viewpoint: H. Landis Gabel and Carl F. Cargill. Gabel argues that standards are only one way to achieve compatibility, and that any discussion of compatibility across products must take account of the effect that any single solution will have on the market itself. Thus imposing a standard, whether formal or informal, will affect the market balance in favour of some and to the detriment of others. The lack of success of many standards initiatives is often a result of a failure to appreciate this.

Cargill, developing his ideas from an IT perspective, offers a similar argument and caveat on standardization. But he also presents a typology of standards, underlying which is a development from product-based to process-based standardization.

While both Gabel and Cargill are correct to emphasize these wider aspects of standardization, there is also a need to analyse the internal preparedness of organizations with regard to innovation and adoption of standards. This leads on to the concept of maturity in the later chapters.

3 STANDARDS AND MATURITY

The market-based arguments of Gabel and Cargill fail to account for the enormous imbalances that exist in the markets themselves. In the IS/IT realm these imbalances are particularly marked, and many of the attempts to develop and impose standards have failed as a result of the machinations of some of the powerful organizations that dictate developments. In the 1980s the 'villain' was IBM, in the 1990s it is Microsoft, among others.

Whatever the rights and wrongs of this, where standards have developed they have often done so as a result of the efforts of the suppliers and developers rather than of the customers. As a result, standards have tended to focus almost exclusively on product compatibility, and some aspects of development. Only in recent years have the service and demand aspects been attended to. The reason for this has often been given in terms of the 'immaturity' of the IS/IT domain; but the meaning of this term, and its assumption of maturing and growth is often left unstated.

This chapter offers a description of the work on techological maturity ranging from Gibson and Nolan's model (1970s) to the 1990s development of 'maturity models' from Humphreys and his colleagues. The differing levels of the various models are used as a basis to confirm the critical importance of standards for organizational maturity, and to discuss the different types of standards that organizations can consider at different stages of growth. This is complemented by a section on a model of individual competence, since the successful adoption and use of standards is dependent as much on individual levels of skill and expertise as it is on the organizational culture and preparedness.

4 STANDARDS FOR SERVICE AND QUALITY IN INFORMATION SYSTEMS ENGINEERING

Discussion of standards inevitably leads to discussion of 'quality'. This chapter offers a brief guide to some of the current quality standards applicable to software development and information systems.

Particular stress is put on a very full and vivid view of quality in IS—not simply a product-based view, but one which also incorporates process and service issues. These aspects are brought together by the introduction of the concept of a *quality horizon*.

An account of some of the key standards initiatives in this area includes an introduction to the SPICE programme which emanates from the maturity work mentioned in Chapter 3.

5 THE DEVELOPMENT OF THE SSADM STANDARD— PART I: FROM INCEPTION TO PREPARATION OF THE DRAFT FOR PUBLIC COMMENT

Chapters 5 and 6 trace the development of the SSADM standard. Chapter 5 gives a brief overview of the development of SSADM, and then covers the early stages of the standardization work, including the initial discussions which took place to determine the type and content of the standard. This first phase ended with the publication of the Draft for Public Comment (DPC) in 1991.

6 THE DEVELOPMENT OF THE SSADM STANDARD— PART II: RESPONDING TO THE DPC, AND EVENTUAL PUBLICATION

The responses to the publication of the DPC caused a fundamental revision of the standard. The newly convened panel was keen to ensure that whatever appeared as the SSADM standard was fit for purpose and clearly presented to the SSADM and wider methods community. This chapter charts the changes to the standard from 1991 to 1993, explaining the reasoning behind the developments. It concludes with an overview of the standard (BS7738) as published in June 1994.

1

WHAT ARE STANDARDS?
WHY STANDARDIZE?

Standards? Out of date? Of course they are, otherwise they wouldn't be
standards.
(adapted from *40 Years On*, Alan Bennett)

In this chapter formal, *de jure* standards are defined, and the definition is
then used to examine the process of standardization, and some aspects of the
motivations leading to standards development.

WHAT ARE STANDARDS?

The central focus for formal, *de jure* standards in the UK is the British
Standards Institution (BSI). Its most discernible manifestation is its
published range of British Standards. These are all referenced by the
letters 'BS', followed by a number. The most fundamental of these standards
is BS0 'A standard for standards'. The current edition dates from 1991, and
this is the third edition of the standard. The standard opens with a statement
of scope, and includes a definition of a standard.

BS0 (1991) defines a standard as a:

Document, established by consensus and approved by a recognized body, that
provides, for common and repeated use, rules, guidelines or characteristics for
activities or their results, aimed at the achievement of the optimum degree of order
in a given context.

An explanatory note states that 'Standards should be based on the consolidated results of science, technology and experience, and aimed at the promotion of optimum community benefits' (BS0, 1991, Part 1, p. 3).

In its previous (1981) edition, the BS0 definition was as follows:

> A technical specification or other document available to the public, drawn up with the cooperation and consensus or general approval of all interests affected by it, based on the consolidated results of science, technology and experience, aimed at the promotion of optimum community benefits and approved by a body recognized on the national, regional or international level.

The scope clause in BS0 qualifies the 1991 definition in stating that this part of BS0 (there are three parts in all) *'describes the general aims and principles of standardization and the use of standards in support of contracts and legislation'* (BS0, 1991, Part 1, p. 3—my italics).

This mention of legal and contractual issues should not detract from the wider aspects invoked by the mention of 'experience', 'community benefits', and the like in both definitions. Although certain standards must have formal, *de jure* status, the full range of standards relevant to IS issues must support far more than simply 'contracts and legislation' if they are genuinely to contribute to an 'optimum degree of order' as stated above.

Later chapters deal specifically with these wider and more diverse aspects of standards. But it is important not to segregate formally published standards from less explicit *de facto* ones (see Appendix). Many of the features that are necessary for an effective standard apply to all types of standard. Standards of every kind—formally published and invoked, or internally distributed within an institution, or range of organizations—have to be understood and examined within an initially common framework. It is also the case that in the area of IS even internal standards will have ramifications beyond the boundaries of any particular organization— particularly as outsourcing, connectivity, networking, and so on become more common.

What of the idea of a standard in a general sense? Originally the term meant a measure, against which other, similar things could be compared. BS0 (1991, Part 1, p. 3) distinguishes between *'etalons'* (measurement standards), and *'normes'* (documentary standards), implying that modern usage entails more than the original concept of measurement and a basis for comparison. This is borne out in the thesaurus supplied with a 'standard' wordprocessing package, which offers the following possibilities:

- *criterion, gauge, measure*—all implying qualitative comparison (hereafter this category will be referred to as 'qualitative comparison').
- *requirement, touchstone, archetype, ideal, model, pattern*—all implying an objective (desired) to be achieved or an end-product to be developed (hereafter 'desired objective').

- *norm, ordinary, usual, average, conventional, orthodox, regular*—all implying consistency, predictability, within expectations (hereafter 'consistent and predictable expectation').
- *banner, ensign, flag, pennant*—a somewhat more archaic use of the term, but still of some relevance (hereafter 'banner').

These alternatives cover a wide variety of concepts, some of them inherently contradictory—for example, a standard as an ideal, and a standard as something ordinary. The thesaurus is correct, however, in offering this range, since it reflects the extent of (mis)understanding of the term itself, not only as part of general opinion, where it is excusable, but also within communities of technical practitioners, where such misapprehensions might seriously damage performance, as well as the effectiveness and derivation of standards themselves.

The BSI definition encompasses many of these ideas, even some of the contradictory ones. (Although let me hasten to add that I cannot offer any better alternative at present.) Standards are envisaged as documents, possibly textual, but perhaps technical in content. In the 1981 edition, they were assumed to take the form of specifications, with the term used in the traditional engineering sense of a model or representation. Like many other terms generalized from engineering, the application and use of 'specification' in the context of software and IS is distinct from its original meaning, and in some instances may be completely misleading. For an engineer a specification may be understood as a blueprint or model; but this is not the meaning appropriate to IS, where a specification may be far nearer to the finished product, as well as a key product in itself, and a component of the final delivered product. (Later we shall see that these considerations on the term 'specification' are critically relevant when looking at different types of standard.) In the period since 1981, the term 'specification' has taken on these new resonances from the context of software development. Thus the 1990 version of BS0 refers merely to a document: the concept of a standard as a specification has disappeared, almost certainly influenced by the use of the term in its expanded software sense.

Orienting discussion around the first three groups of meanings of the term—qualitative comparison; desired objective; consistent and predictable expectation—is a useful starting point in considering the nature of standards. The relevance of any one or more of the three distinct meanings will emanate from the motivation behind the development and use of any single standard or range of standards.

A standard designed primarily to be a qualitative comparison will be one that will have to include a measurement basis for determining compliance. Any candidate for certification against the standard will have to be assessed in terms of the rating of one or more of its characteristics against that of the 'standard'. Whether the result can exceed 100 per cent, or whether there is a tolerance of achieving less than 100 per cent will vary according to the standard itself. Examples of such standards would be those relating to material strength or flexibility, or to some readily measurable aspect of performance or provision.

Developing a standard as a desired objective, or 'ideal', is a more enigmatic endeavour. This meaning of the term owes more to common everyday usage than to the more restricted sense here. We might all wish to live up to some ideal standard of behaviour or achievement, but we would be affronted if someone else sought to measure our actual attempts against the ideal, and then pointed out our shortcomings. In this interpretation of the word, a standard is almost certainly an unattainable level of perfection, but should encourage a striving for improvement and enhancement. This is fine in an informal and localized context. But if a more formal standard is seen as unrealizable it may simply become unworkable or irrelevant. This has always been the danger in developing 'quality' standards, although the current range of such standards (BS5750/ISO9000, etc.) clearly addresses the issue of 'what to do next' rather than that of defining a utopian ideal.

On the other hand, a standard in the sense defined by BS0 can be seen as an ideal in the way that it should become the desired objective for relevant practitioners or developers: a standard as encouraging or embodying 'best practice'. But this 'best' must not be an impossible level of perfection.

The concept of a standard as a 'consistent and predictable expectation' is the one most applicable to the present context. In this connotation a standard affords a basis for planning and control—an aspect critical to the domain of IS issues and concerns. The next chapter will examine the application of this meaning of a standard to the realm of ISs.

BS0, while not offering a distinction between the different meanings of standard as outlined above, does go some way to clarify the term in its classification of differing types of standard.

British Standards can take the following forms, e.g.:

a) specifications for products or materials: dimensions, performance, safety, etc.; specifications for processes, practices, systems, etc.;
b) methods of measuring, testing, analysing, specifying, etc.;
c) recommendations on product or process applications; codes of practice;
d) terminology, symbols;
e) classification.   (BS0, Part 3, p. 6)

These are each defined (BS0, Part 3, Section 2.1) as follows:

BS specifications lay down requirements to be satisfied by a product, material, process or system, together with the methods by which conformity may be verified.

BS methods formalize ways of doing things.

BS codes of practice recommend good, accepted practice for the accomplishment of a defined task. They are advisory, not intended to provide objective criteria by which compliance may be judged.

BS glossaries define and standardize terminology, often in association with units, symbols and conventions. Classifications have the same status as glossaries; their function is to designate and describe different grades of product or arrange data in an agreed hierarchical order.

From the earlier discussion concerning 'tangibility' across the range of IS, standards in the form of specifications would most readily apply to the hardware and communications platforms. Standards in the form of methods would be more appropriate for the less tangible aspects of the system. (In the next chapter, and later in the detailed account of the development of the SSADM standard, this assertion will be discussed more fully.)

Since there are several different types of standard, there ought to be criteria for deciding which type is most suitable for any particular context. This focuses attention on the process of developing standards: standardization. People have to converge and agree not only to develop a standard, but to do so in a specified format and aiming at a particular type of standard.

Again BS0 provides a reference point, defining 'standardization' (in the prior section to that defining a standard) as the 'activity of establishing, with regard to actual or potential problems, provisions for common and repeated use, aimed at the achievement of the optimum degree of order in a given context' (BS0, p. 3). Two explanatory notes are appended to this definition. The first states that 'the activity consists of the processes of formulating, issuing and implementing standards'. The second that 'important benefits of standardization are improvement of the suitability of products, processes and services for their intended purposes, prevention of barriers to trade and facilitation of technological cooperation'.

This resonates with all the three meanings of standard discussed earlier. Improvements in products, processes, and services can only be accomplished if there is some yardstick (standard) against which improvement can be assessed—qualitative comparison. This striving for improvement is also in tune with the concept of achieving a desired objective. The points concerning more open trade and enhanced co-operation align with the meaning of standards as providing a framework of consistent and predictable expectations.

It is no coincidence that in BS0 the process of standardization is defined before standards themselves. The activity is critical: without sufficient attention to its intentions and objectives, the development of standards would be a pointless exercise. If standards are to reflect genuine, informed consensus, then the process of standardization must ensure that this consensus can evolve. Standards have to emerge and endure as a result of a genuine and sustained need. The process of creating and developing standards must be centred around discerning and eliciting requirements for specific standards or groups of standards. (Although we all need to take warning from Cargill that the ability to participate in standards making is 'less a function of technical ability than it is of endurance' —Cargill, 1989, p. 68.)

WHY ARE STANDARDS NEEDED?

Standards are needed for a variety of reasons, some of which are implied in the definitions of standardization already given, and in the discussion of standards themselves. They can provide a basis for order, affording a platform for innovation, development, and general planning. This may be particularly important in a rapidly changing, technologically based realm such as IS. With regard to the technical equipment itself, it is critical, given that manufacturers and suppliers often specialize in particular items. In the short term and narrow view, producers may be content with binding their customers to their own selected range of attachments; but in the long term even the most coercive-minded producer/supplier will see the benefit of an open basis for customer selection. After all, unless the producer has a monopoly or near monopoly, a 'closed' market may bind in a segment of the consumers to one supplier, but it will also preclude others bound to alternative sources.

This is a critical point, since it may otherwise be believed that standards are beneficial for consumers and wholly detrimental and constraining for developers/suppliers. The lesson of the development of the personal computer indicates that at least in part the industry itself was a key player in the adoption of the *de facto* standard of the IBM PC (see below). The IBM PC became a standard in the sense of providing a consistent and predictable expectation. Once this was established and accepted it became a force in itself, even if it is not of *de jure* status. Technically this may not be desirable since the material embodiment of this 'consistent and predictable expectation' may not be the best possible solution, either leading up to the time it was so established or later as other developments occur. In serving to stabilize and harmonize an incoherent domain, however, it may enable a range of benefits to accrue, serving the interests of producer/supplier and consumer; although how the overall benefit is shared may be a contested matter. (Again the IBM PC serves as an example—see below.)

If we accept that standards can play a key role in the development and preservation of order and repeatability, then they will be needed in any domain in which the hierarchy of planning, organization, and control is weak or insubstantial, e.g. IS. This is not to say that the realization that planning and management are futile or ineffectual will immediately result in a focus on standards as a contributor to the solution. But in fact the emergence of standards—whether *de facto* or *de jure*—will tend to occur precisely because such a development will resolve some of the problems. The actual resilience, extent, form, and content of the standards will be context dependent, and related to the maturity and market division of the domain—as will be shown in later chapters.

This helps us go some way to answering the question 'why are standards needed?' They are needed because they will afford some basis for planning and predictability, and order—a much sought-after commodity.

In the next chapter the discussion of the need for standards will be oriented more specifically to the IS realm, but for now it should simply be noted that the most conventional rationale given for developing standards is that they facilitate a 'common interchange'. Other (partially related) reasons include mention of the benefits of standards as the striving for greater safety, interchangeability, risk reduction, and integration of technological advances.

This is not to say that the reason given for the development of any particular standard will always be couched in these terms. There may be numerous justifications for a specific standard. But in general, people will look for and adhere to standards primarily if they satisfy the demand for regularity and predictability.

Given that standards will be envisaged as necessary or desirable requirements in arbitrary and unstable contexts in which planning and predictability are haphazard, and where there is a demand for compatibility and interchange, then what might be the common route to the development of a formal standard? Cargill (1989) castigates those who indulge in a 'rush to standards', which often characterizes fields of endeavour that have become chaotic and disorganized.

This often overdue search for an elusive panacea is bound to prove illusory. Cargill himself points out that it is an unsatisfactory basis upon which to develop standards, and betrays a mistaken view of standards and the standards-making process—misconceptions that emanate from both the academic community and standards bodies themselves. Standards must not be seen as a simple solution to awkward problems, nor as a universally applicable solution.

Essentially the formal statement of a standard must represent a milestone in a process that starts with recognition of a problem of co-ordination between parties. Without the problem existing there would be no need for a standard. Without some level or form of mutual recognition that there is a problem, there is little hope that a meaningful, relevant, and implementable standard can be developed.

This then goes much of the way to answering the fundamental question 'how does the need for standards arise?' Standards are needed when there is some mutual realization of a problem of co-ordination. But this is not to imply that in such cases standards are the only solution as Gabel (1991) has pointed out (see below).

This necessity for mutual understanding, taken together with the importance of consensus and common interest, might lead to an impression that standards develop in a harmonious and balanced fashion. Some may well do so, emerging from shared conceptions of the common good; others, however, only arise as a result of the endeavours of a regulatory body seeking to impose some measure of consistency and uniformity on its province of activity. This is a concept of standard more akin to rule or regulation than to any of the meanings discussed previously. Within any single organization the imposition of such a stipulation may be warranted and achievable. In an open and less regulated context a more mediated approach is both required and realistic.

In relation to the IS arena, subject as it is to a wide variety of potentially divisive commercial pressures, the only workable standards will be those based on consensus. As Gray concludes in her discussion of the profound economic rationale for open systems based on standards in the IT industry, the balance between effective utilization of the technology and innovation and competitiveness is 'through the adoption of international, widely used, consensus standards for IT systems, supported by the entire computer industry, and set in such a way as to reflect the real needs and priorities of the marketplace' (Gray, 1991, p. 5). Which is all fine, but rather begs the question of how such a situation can be achieved and sustained.

The theme that arises continually in recent discussions of standards, particularly with regard to IS/IT, is the inevitable combination of technical control and market mechanisms. This insistence on the importance of the market is well founded. We are now at the stage where interest in the development of national standards may well decline, based on the assumption that national standards are inherently barriers to international competition. Conversely international standards are regarded as intrinsic stimulators of international trade and competition, providing effective bases for regulation of these activities, and simultaneously affording expanded markets for supplier organizations.

As markets become predominantly international or transnational, the demand for international standards will grow. *De facto* international standards emerged almost effortlessly in freight containerization, since this was by definition an international concern. The rapid development of international standards for communications also exemplifies this combination of supplier-led and demand-led impetus (although other industry-specific factors also played an important part, as Gray [1991] explains). On the other hand, there is little point developing an international standard unless there is an international market, and there may well be national forces working against such moves.

In the development of television, however, initially standards developed nationally since the technology preceded the expansion of transborder communications technology. This later influenced the format for videos, and has meant that 'universal' products have had to emerge which can bridge across different 'standard' formats. The 'need' had to accommodate the existing technology and standards already in place. In later chapters this will be seen to be equally applicable to the IS realm, once some standards have been developed.

ESTABLISHING A NEED FOR A STANDARD

Standards will appear and operate most successfully if they satisfy or stimulate a real need. How can these needs be discovered and articulated? Since not all needs will be satisfied by standards, is there some formal mechanism for gauging standards needs? Or do these needs simply emerge into the specialist or public realm by some mysterious process?

In some cases the need for a particular standard may be clearly understood and accepted before the standard itself is devised. A case in point would be the RS232 interface, which arose from the paramount need for what we now term 'plug compatibility' at a fundamental level between a variety of machines performing a range of complementary functions—specifically computers and printers. This is a good example of a standard as a consistent and predictable expectation. It benefits all main interests, including consumers and suppliers of printers, computers, and software. Perhaps the only ones it disadvantaged were those who wanted to constrain consumer choice within tightly bundled packages of hardware and software, and those offering consultancy services for linking product 'X' running on machine 'Y' to printer 'Z'.

Compare this with the situation of 'plug non-compatibility' for everyday electrical appliances. Since there was already a well-entrenched variety of electrical socket types in the UK by the 1970s, the 'need' for a standard was in conflict with the practical issues that would have been involved in imposing a single socket type. No consensus was achievable. The situation was 'resolved' for many years by simply not supplying plugs with appliances: consistent and predictable, at least to those with experience of UK conventions. (North Americans in particular always found it profoundly shocking that an electrical appliance could exist, let alone be sold, without a plug.) In the 1990s, with almost universal adoption of a single socket type in the UK, many retailers now supply 'standard' plugs with the appliance. In this case the standard could only emerge once a levelling up to newer technology had become near universal. This may not always be possible, particularly if the technologies run in parallel, rather than in sequence. This can confound even those charged with responsibilities for international trade and exchange. Hence the bizarre vision of the UK Trade and Industry Secretary in the 1980s, who spoke of the open market of the EC providing the possibility of buying a television in the UK, a videocassette recorder in Germany, and connecting them in France—completely oblivious to the fundamental incompatibilities at numerous levels from electrical mains operation to television encoding. ('Three impossible things before breakfast TV', as Lewis Carroll might have put it.)

In general the development of a standard is as likely to be forestalled by existing interests, market segmentation, and investments in technology and other resources, as it is to be stymied by the introduction of new technologies and skills. With regard to IS/IT, with both sets of factors playing significant roles, it is perhaps not surprising that standards development is uneven and haphazard: in some respects it is remarkable that any standards have developed at all.

In most situations, however, it may not even be clear that a standard is the solution to a problem or set of problems—in which case there may be several opposing positions, and the argument for a standard will have to be articulated and won. This cannot be done effectively by adopting an initial strategy based on identifying needs for standards. This would be tantamount to establishing a code of rules for a game, and only then investigating if the game exists and is being played, or is worthwhile inventing. Put in these terms, such an orientation may appear ridiculous, but unfortunately it is not an uncommon one in the standards-making world, where there are many 'standards professionals' who no longer see standards as a means to an end, but as ends in themselves.

Realistically the identification of needs for standards can only be an indirect activity. Initially there must be some agreement on the range and type of issues demanding resolution in a given domain. If these include the necessity for some basis for planning, organization, and control, and for integration of a range of disparate products or services, then standards will be worth consideration. Only then can potential solutions be considered, including the possible role to be played by standards.

At a fundamental level, standards contribute to orderliness and predictability. As Marciniak and Reifer state 'standards play a stabilizing role because they allow organizations to communicate in common terms within a decision framework that everyone understands' (1990, p. 33). But this may have to be achieved at the cost of severely constraining change, and perhaps putting monopoly power in the hands of a small segment of the market, or in extreme cases of a single supplier. In the past this role was clearly taken by IBM; the obvious example now is the dominant role of Microsoft in the PC market, specifically with its bundling of MS-DOS and Windows.

Thus standards permit common interchange across issues such as planning, prediction, control, and repeatability, thereby permitting skill development and re-use, resource flexibility, communication, and a variety of linkages to other activities, aspects, and functions. Sometimes it is sufficient that such mechanisms can be achieved internally or informally, but once the scale of interests extends significantly, the effect of a 'standard' on the market can have serious effects and can actually reduce competition and openness.

The argument for formal *de jure* standards is that they at least counteract such tendencies by taking the specification into the public domain, thereby permitting a wider degree of competition. The example of the emerging PCI standard discussed in Chapter 2 is an example of this process at work.

One test for a standard being truly required is that it should be possible to envisage a subeconomy developing around its enforcement, implementation, certification, etc. This is essentially arguing that for a standard to operate effectively there must be people willing to pay for its enforcement and certification—i.e. who see the standard as providing them with a net benefit. This is a useful test against which many current standards developments should be assessed.

HOW ARE STANDARDS DEVISED AND DEFINED?

Assuming that the need for a standard has been established, it is important to clarify the type of standard and its scope. Standards can apply to products, processes, and resources. They can be publicly owned or privately controlled. They can have *de jure* status or operate as *de facto* standards. Gabel, in his analysis of product standards, offers a distinction between proprietary and public domain standards (Gabel, 1991, ch. 1): the former are available either on restricted or open access. Thus the IBM PC was an open proprietary standard; that for PS/2 was initially meant to be restricted. It can also be pointed out that the public domain standards can be either formally recognized, i.e. published by an authorized standards body, or less formally acknowledged as a standard in some sense by those with relevant interests. As will be shown in later chapters, SSADM was already an informal standard within certain UK confines, even before the work on the British Standard for SSADM was initiated.

The actual formulation of a standard is ostensibly performed by small groups of individuals with the necessary characteristics of expertise, experience, and enthusiasm—all under the jurisdiction of a standards institution. In fact most standards committees include some such individuals, but also a large proportion of contributors representing group interests, both supplier and consumer. Although the official definitions of standardization rightly stress the need for openness and consensus, the process of developing a formal standard also demands significant resources and some form of sponsor or champion prepared to motivate others and foster the required efforts. In this sense the standards marketplace is as uneven and unequal as any other marketplace.

The initial work on standards will then tend to emerge from expressions of group interests. These may be demands for regulation or certification of specific activities. They may arise from requirements to control change, allow access to new domains, or challenge a monopoly. As later chapters will show, the insistence on a standard may cause constraints in development, or encourage particular forms of innovation. There is no easy explanation to account for the full range of standards motivations, although some of those associated with product standards are covered in Gabel's (1991) discussion.

Some organizations have at their disposal sufficient resources to fund the development of standards almost to the point of completion. Other standards require the attraction of resources from a variety of contexts, and hence have to be marketed. But in both cases if a true *de jure* standard is to emerge, some formal decision to proceed will be needed from an authorizing body. Until relatively recently this would have been a national standards body, or occasionally a trade association of some sort. Increasingly, transnational bodies are taking on this role. National standards are in many fields gradually being replaced by international standards, sometimes the latter being transcriptions of the former. Thus the original UK quality standard, BS5750, formed the basis of the international version ISO9000. The current version of BS5750 is simply the UK edition of ISO9000, and control of the standard is now vested with the relevant international body and not with the BSI.

Once the necessary critical mass of interest and resources has been assembled, the statement of the standard can be developed. Although there is perhaps no inherent reason why all formal standards should be primarily textual documents, they almost always are. Thus the drafting of a document forms the largest proportion of the development work at this stage, although in some cases large parts of the standard may be reworkings of existing documents or specifications (as was the case with SSADM). Standards can range in size and complexity from just a few paragraphs to several volumes and additional technical annexes.

Whatever its eventual size and scope, a standard must be readable and usable by its intended audience; and to a large extent it must be self-contained, not requiring access to additional material or documentation, particularly if that material is itself not immediately available to the public. This constraint can lead to some misunderstanding, as will be demonstrated in the example of the SSADM experience, but the idea is sound as it should ensure that standards are fully available for use, and not simply a partial statement giving public credence to what remains a proprietary feature under private control.

It is perfectly reasonable to refer to other publications, and especially to other standards. The BSI makes the distinction between normative and informative references. Thus the former, usually applied to other standards or accessible specifications, implies that the material contained in those documents is encompassed by the clauses of the standard. Informative references, on the other hand, do not have this force.

Once completed, the draft text will then be distributed for comment. There may be more than one stage of draft documentation, but at each point copies will be made available to representatives on standards bodies, and various announcements will be made with details of the document, sources from where it can be obtained, and the date by which comments must be received. At the international level comments need to emanate from a national standards body, at lower levels individuals and informal groups may respond, as may other more official bodies. The ultimate objective of such soundings of opinion is the achievement of total consensus, but there is no entirely satisfactory mechanism for ensuring that all those likely to be affected by the standard have been consulted.

Reactions to drafts will tend to be a combination of positive responses, a large number of null responses, and a few responses largely encouraging, but pointing out some inconsistencies, ambiguities, or omissions. In a few instances there may be one or more vigorously negative responses, in which case there has to be a mechanism that seeks to resolve the conflict, but permits some way forward even if such a settlement cannot be derived. If the reason for objecting to a draft standard arises from fundamental disagreement with the idea of such a standard itself, then the opposing party may be in a position simply to choose to ignore the standard once it becomes recognized. This happens sometimes with international standards, where one country refuses to endorse a standard. On the other hand, if the disagreement focuses on the content of the standard, then there may be a split that ultimately brings discredit onto the entire activity of standards themselves. The development of various international standards for some programming languages and repository structures illustrates this. In some cases reactions have been sufficiently adverse to prevent the further development of the standard.

OPERATING A STANDARD

Assuming some consensus can be achieved, and the standard published, there needs to be some administrative framework for the operation of the standard. This must cover publication, distribution, and revision as a bare minimum. Most standards published recently have a five-year revision cycle, at the end of which a deliberate decision must be taken to withdraw, revise, or reconfirm the publication. Other aspects of standards concern such topics as enforcement, adjudication between varying interpretations, scope, coverage, and relevance. The relationship between standards and legal obligations, particularly those contained in contractual documents, has often been misconstrued. One of the mistakes often made with regard to standards in general is that people believe that whatever is published in an official standard has a mandatory application where relevant. This is not the case, as BS0 clearly states:

> British Standards are publicly available documents voluntarily agreed as a result of processes of public consultation designed to secure public acceptance. However, the publication of a standard by BSI does not, in itself, ensure its use. Its application depends on the voluntary action of interested parties. It becomes binding if it is made mandatory by legislation, if a party is contracted to work to it or once claim of compliance with it has been made.   (BS0, Part 1, Section 3.1.1)

Apart from specific instances where additional regulations or legal stipulations apply, the decision to apply a standard rests entirely with the contractual parties. Moreover simply quoting a standard does not suffice: 'It remains the responsibility of users to ensure that a particular standard is appropriate to their needs' (Section 3.1.3).

The control of the application and extent of standards is not performed by the standards bodies themselves. But these bodies may become involved in conflicts over application and interpretation between disputants or litigants. Indeed, if the standard itself is found wanting, and hence a cause of the complaint, the committee responsible for the document may itself become a party to the dispute.

The overall point to bear in mind is that a published standard is one component of a negotiating context, it is not the source of detailed rules for arriving at a satisfactory agreement. Standards cannot replace intelligence, thoughtfulness, and compromise: but then what can?

HOW ARE STANDARDS LIMITED BY NATIONAL FRONTIERS?

Currently the standards world is in a state of flux, particularly in the European Union (EU). Most national countries have a standards body, and most standards bodies are affiliated to the respective international body. With the increase in international trade, in both products and services, the necessity for a coherent and usable range of international standards has become more urgent. Moreover, the existence of national standards in some of these areas has proved a hindrance to such trading. The most cosmopolitan solution to this would be for all national and partisan standards to be rescinded in favour of international analogues. This is unlikely to happen, since the derivation of standards exhibits the common 80:20 split; in this case with 80 per cent being the political considerations, and 20 per cent the technical. Thus national standards remain an important focus of attention, for both positive and negative reasons. Gradual realignments, and counterparts to the development of ISO9000, will ensure that some truly international standards do emerge, but that will only ever be part of the picture.

The context is, however, rendered more complex with the evolution of a EU standards policy, together with accompanying EU standards (EN— European Normes). This means that for any EU member state there could potentially be three conflicting standards: national, European, and international. An organization trading internally might have to comply with the national standard. It might have to comply with the European one for EU-based trade, and with the ISO one for the remainder. The result would be confusion and chaos; or would mean that no standards were invoked.

Such an option is not available in the public sector, since in many cases certain standards are mandatory. Thus the current position in the EU is that in such cases any relevant EU standard must be invoked. If none applies, then an international standard can be applied, and in the absence of either of these, a national standard can be used, although only in certain circumstances (see Chapter 6).

This is only partially satisfactory when one considers what might happen if numerous standards were to be required in a public procurement exercise extending across several borders. The eventual agreement might need to reference national, European, and international standards, and clarify the relationships between them. No doubt, in most cases the parties to the agreement would be able to resolve such matters; and in time perhaps a code of practice would be produced to guide people through the complications. At present, however, the situation is fraught with misunderstanding and difficulties and is unlikely to be remedied by formal guidance from the relevant bodies.

The pressures for ever-wider market access, combined with the legitimacy afforded to legal frameworks preventing monopolies and cartels, will result in increased demands for effective and enforceable international standards. Such standards may not necessarily emerge solely through the deliberations of standards bodies. Indeed what is certainly one of the most important standards in IS/IT emerged in a wholly different way, but its development still demonstrates some of the important features of standards already mentioned.

THE IBM PC—AN EXAMPLE OF SOME ASPECTS OF STANDARDS DEVELOPMENT

The development of the personal computer is an interesting example of some of the points developed in this chapter, in the context of a product that is now regarded as a standard, and which has in turn prompted the development of many *de jure* standards.

The pressures that led to the IBM PC becoming the *de facto* standard emanated as much from other suppliers as from consumers. IBM's near monopoly position in one very visible segment of the computer market, led to its own, possibly inferior product becoming the standard offering. There were many PC-type platforms around in the middle to late 1970s. Indeed IBM, having ignored the minicomputer market for many years, appeared to be adopting the same attitude with regard to PCs. Eventually, however, in 1980 the IBM PC appeared. Once launched, the product was destined to provide a focus for standardization purely on the basis of it being IBM's offering. Just as many companies had thrived on producing IBM-compatible hardware and software for mainframes, so now many saw the opportunity of reaching a large market on the back of IBM's efforts. Developers of software and PC peripherals were as needful of a 'standard' platform for their products and services as were consumers for a stable product which afforded a sound investment in terms of durability and scope for enhancement.

Many of the IBM PC's predecessors, developed at great risk by less well known or completely new companies, simply disappeared: the criteria of survival or demise bore little or no correlation with technical capability. By the mid-1980s the IBM PC had become a generic product, copied by many and significantly improved by a few. It had thus become a 'standard' in the sense of a consistent and predictable expectation. Once this position is established in a well-understood and delineated domain, the standard becomes a force in itself, even if it is not of *de jure* status. Technically this may not be desirable since the material embodiment of this 'consistent and predictable expectation' may not be the best possible solution, either leading up to the time it was so established or later as other developments occur. In serving to stabilize and harmonize an incoherent domain, however, it may enable a range of benefits to accrue, serving the interests of producer/supplier and consumer—although how the overall benefit is shared may be a contested matter.

The later developments around the IBM PC illustrate this. By the late 1980s the *IBM* PC was practically free of its parent company to the extent that when IBM did try to launch a new model more tightly associated with IBM itself (PS/2) it foundered, in part due to its incompatibility with the existing standard itself.

But what would have happened if the weight of IBM had not been a key feature? What if there was no single dominant market contender? After all, the appearance of a *de jure* standard in this fashion is probably the exception rather than the norm. This would even be true of slightly less monopolistic situations, such as that of the contention over videocassette format that occurred between the three or four major manufacturers in the 1980s. (It might be noted that this also occurred, but to a lesser extent, in the case of audiocassette versus audiocartridge—remember them?—format; but did not occur in, for instance, freight containerization. This is an example of the argument that the more mature the industry, the easier is some semblance and actuality of standardization—an argument examined in Chapter 3.)

Gabel (1991) points to several possibilities in such cases. Either a standard of some sort emerges, backed by large consortia with sufficient purchasing power to pressure suppliers; or perhaps a small number of possibilities emerge combined with additional *gateway* products enabling transfer or interconnection (see Chapter 2). He correctly distinguishes between multi-vendor and multi-vintage compatibility; and the strength of the IBM PC as a standard is that to a very large extent it offers both. Furthermore, successors to some aspects of the original PC environment have had to take on this dual compatibility in order to maximize their appeal, e.g. Windows.

What distinguishes some aspects of the IBM PC story from standards in general is that the IS/IT realm is far newer and less stable than many others. The next chapter considers what this entails, together with its impact on the process of standardization for products and other aspects of IS.

2

STANDARDS AND STANDARDIZATION IN THE IS/ISE DOMAIN

Having considered some general issues relating to standards and standardization, it is now time to turn to some of the features specific to the realm of software engineering and information systems. In this computer-related area there is much justified scepticism regarding standards. As a fairly recent survey of IT standards put it: 'Every firm wants a monopoly—and every firm wants to call it an open standard' (*Economist*, 27 February 1991). The response to this might be a total scepticism with regard to standards, or the belief that standards will fail to materialize, but it is important to realize that in one form or another standards will emerge. These need not necessarily be overt, *de jure* standards, but could be *de facto* standards, most commonly supplier enforced. Or they could even be the product of consumer pressure, most likely consolidated through an effective users' group.

In practice many of the most obvious 'standards' in the IT field are precisely those where a firm has managed to achieve a near-monopoly for a particular component or design or technology, and others have then adopted it, or adapted to it, as if it were a standard in the sense of a basis for common interchange or interface. This then permits developments in the associated technologies to extend from a defined basis. It might be argued that this constrains innovation, but at least it offers a foundation and target for subsequent innovation. On the other hand, if the result is 'a defined and accessible basis for development' then it can serve as a standard in the full sense.

The real problems arise when there is a 'standard product' that is still owned and protected by one company. In such circumstances the benefits of a standard have to be weighed against the costs and imbalances of a monopoly. The previous dominance of IBM, and the current arguments around the position of Microsoft, are examples of this tension: opponents contend that these organizations have achieved the position described in the above quote from the *Economist*.

Since the IT area has always been one in which investment has been substantial, and increasingly where the rate of technological change has been immense, the demand for standards that afford a consistent and predictable expectation in this manner is not surprising. Controlled innovation may be constrained and constraining, but at least it permits technology users to plan incremental upgrades and incorporation of new functionality and facilities without the fear of complete obsolescence of existing investments in skill and resources. As later chapters will show, through examples such as Gibson and Nolan's work, apart from a brief initiation period, there has been a continuous demand for control and assessment of IT expenditure, and standards can be a factor in satisfying this demand.

In fact control in any form, such as a standard architecture or product range, will prove beneficial both to consumers and suppliers, although it may preclude those with innovations classified as not conforming with the standard. In such cases a rival range of products may emerge, with its own 'standards'.

This all results in what can be termed the 'paradox of IS standardization'. The combination of high levels of investment with an accelerating rate of change produces an urgent demand for standards of some sort; yet this very combination also impedes the development of a context from which the consensus or general approval for standardization strategies can emerge.

THE PARADOX OF IS STANDARDIZATION

The greatest need for standardization almost always arises in the realm in which the consensus required for the emergence of standards is likely to prove the most difficult to attain. This is a paradox clearly exemplified in IS/IT. In IT particularly it was also the case that some of the early attempts to standardize fell foul of the immense developments in the technology, particularly those that offered price/performance ratios improved by several orders of magnitude over periods of a few years. Any cost-saving potential from a standard was rapidly eroded by such developments.

But this is not to argue that even in such frenzied contexts standards in some form will not emerge. The choice is never between standards developing or failing to develop; it is between them evolving in a relatively rational and consensual fashion, or in a piecemeal, impositional, and unanticipated one. In a non-standardized open market, dominant suppliers will seek to establish their own products or services as standards, compelling consumers to make portentous and risky decisions with highly imperfect information. This constrains their choices for both the present and the future.

In such circumstances if no single organization is dominant a supplier cartel may emerge to secure such a position. This might be countered by an equally powerful group of consumer organizations, able to exert influence by the sheer weight of their combined purchasing power. But with the prevailing philosophy of market forces, open competition, and a shrinking role for the public sector, this counterbalance is severely circumscribed and unlikely to be effective in a context as unstable as that around IT and IS. The potential role for standards in IS, then, ought to become a critical one for the embodiment of consumer interests, although it has hardly been recognized as such.

Ironically recognition of the role standards might play in such market contexts has been more prevalent among suppliers, who have realized that with the technology changing so rapidly, they cannot maintain a market edge with any certainty. Even those who do manage to achieve dominance in one form quickly learn that such a position requires a sustained level of activity. As the IBM PC example illustrates, even the company 'owning' the standard may not be able or ready to exploit it to its fullest extent, and may eventually lose market share to other, more effective suppliers of standard equipment.

The PC example also illustrates that even in rapidly developing fields such as IT, a critical mass of consumer pressure can constrain or direct further development. Having made large investments in one level of technology, consumers want realistic upgrade paths even if they preclude some desirable or fanciful enhancements. Although PCs are relatively low-cost items, the overall implications of decisions relating to networks and software are enormous—a factor clearly appreciated by Microsoft, Novell, and others currently battling for stakes in this sector.

But the PC example of consumer-led *de facto* standardization should not be taken as typical. Moreover, the detailed aspects of the PC 'standard' are far from standardized, as anyone who has installed software, printers, and other external devices will attest.

The preceding chapter outlined the case for considering concerns for predictability, control, and repeatability as key motivations for standardization in some form. In the computer-related areas of IS the urge for the development of these supports for management is particularly keenly felt.

Levels of investment in an organization's information system are significant, and the reliance on its operation and performance is now likely to be critical for the continued existence of the organization itself.

Furthermore, almost by definition, purely internal standards (codes of practice, quality, etc.) will be insufficient since the organization's information system extends well beyond the confines of the organization itself. The technology will have to be acquired from a wide variety of sources and specialists, and the skills to operate and develop the system and supporting technology cannot be nurtured and encompassed within even the largest organization. Outsourcing and end-user purchasing simply add other factors to an already complex network of inputs and interdependencies.

Even organizations that consider themselves predominantly suppliers of IS/IT products or services have to try to establish long-term planning and predictability in their IS policies and objectives. These organizations will also need to consider how best to gain appropriate levels of control and evaluation to protect their investments, and guarantee their continued and effective existence. Only a very few organizations can impose their own specific standards on others, or demand them from others, so realistically the main strategic decisions relate to the degree to which some form of regulation and ascendancy can be imposed upon a bewildering present and an uncertain future.

Often the simplest solution appears to be that of finding the relevant bandwagon, and then jumping aboard. Hence once a particular technology has gained a critical mass of adherents it may well succeed purely because there is a sufficiently large customer base. There is at least some safety in numbers. The saying from the 1970s that 'no one ever got fired for buying IBM' still echoes to the 1990s, although it no longer applies to IBM.

Furthermore there is a tempering of any apprehension at making a specific decision with the comfort that at least there will be fellow sufferers from any disastrous consequences. Fortunately in the hardware realm this clustering around a core technology is becoming easier at the base level, both because standard products have emerged, and also because formal international standards have been or are being developed. But this situation is already proving transitory as the technology transforms, and the range and nature of its application develops. In part this is because the 'core' technology is not in fact stable, but spawns extensions that initially are fully compatible, but which eventually outstrip the earliest aspects (see below on the VESA VL-Bus). In addition, the market is potentially so complex and lucrative that organizations with products in one sector will not be content to allow dominance to be maintained by others in related sectors. Thus the current battle between Intel's Pentium and the contending PowerPC of IBM, Sun, *et al.* has as much to do with related products—software, networks, value-added components, etc.—as it has with the chip architecture itself.

The overall result is a 'base' standard with a degree of security and predictability, with certain pressures and restraints on innovation; but this quickly becomes subverted as new components and options result in non-standard supersets. Instead of growth being linear, it branches at certain points relying on critical decisions being taken. This frequently occurs with, for instance, programming languages, where most suppliers, seeking competitive edge, offer enhanced versions of standard products. The effect of this is to present consumers with having to evaluate added functionality against the risk of uncertainty regarding compatibility and future upgrades.

This situation is illustrated by the following example from *PCuser* (July/August 1993).

> Standards are a good thing. They protect users from buying incompatible hardware. Right?
> Well not exactly. Take the VESA Local Bus (VL-Bus). Unlike PCI, it was cobbled together in a hurry and it shows. Page through the computer adverts and you'll soon see 50MHz 486DX PCs claiming to comply with the VESA Local-Bus standard. . . . Compatibility problems are rearing their ugly heads, because some PC vendors are only now beginning to read the VESA specifications for the VL-Bus PCs with accelerated video on expansion cards in 50MHz 486DX PCs they're flogging.   (Editorial, p. 9)

Essentially the standard precludes add-in cards for systems operating above 40 MHz. Manufacturers have 'extended' the standard to produce products with added value, but in so doing have departed from the standard and almost certainly compromised reliability and future compatibility. The editor, Terence Green, contrasts this with the emergence of the Peripheral Component Interconnect (PCI) standard. This was initiated by Intel, who wished to ensure that faster processors would not be hampered by machine design based largely on that of the IBM AT. Intel transferred the PCI development to a committee, and donated all patents to the public domain: 'the PC equivalent of Coca-Cola giving everybody in the world the right to print its logo' (p. 26). This has led so far to a specification that represents and reflects all relevant interests, and will possibly provide a support for future developments in many related features of PC systems. There is still the possibility that the situation of the VL-Bus will be repeated, but at least there is some firmer basis for an agreed framework for advance.

Given the pace of innovation in IT and the overall emergence of IS as a specific realm, it is unfortunate, although perfectly understandable, that across the IS domain as a whole, standards have developed in a haphazard and uneven fashion. Most of the standards that have emerged have done so around the tangible and obvious facets of the technology itself. But even these have often only emerged after a somewhat random and irrational gestation process: the eventual 'standard' often has no obvious technical or strategic advantage other than its provenance and commercial derivation—the IBM PC syndrome.

This is not to undermine standards in the 'IT' area of IS, but rather to indicate that perhaps the existing ones are not necessarily or primarily addressing critical aspects of 'IT', and may not be fit for purpose. On the contrary, standards in IS/IT are critical because of the rapid rate of change; but this, coupled with the very large vested interests makes true standardization complex and demanding. Some informal standards do emerge, but this may be only transitory.

STANDARDS AND COMPATIBILITY

The classic argument in favour of technology-based product standards is that they promote compatibility. This argument is applied even in situations where the 'standard' is a single, dominant supplier's product, e.g. Windows. It is also seen as the basis for establishing competition against a dominant supplier, such as the motivation behind the OSI protocols by those who sought to challenge IBM's mainframe hegemony. This is, however, countered or at least severely qualified by, for instance, Gabel (1991) who points to the ways in which many standards have developed precisely to preclude certain forms of compatibility, or to enforce existing product dominance. Gabel stresses, correctly, that standardization and compatibility are not synonymous—moreover: 'Standardization is often not the best way to achieve compatibility' (1991, p. 172).

It would certainly be generally accepted by all those using IS/IT products and services that compatibility is an unquestioned and primary ambition. Standardization is then a secondary objective, deriving its importance precisely because it promotes compatibility. Gabel's argument is that there are other, possibly more effective, means for achieving the same end. He defines three mechanisms for achieving compatibility, and these are *in competition* with one another. The three are termed respectively compatibility by network competition, by agreement on a 'neutral' standard, and by adoption of gateways.

Compatibility by network competition can be exemplified by the case of the emergence of the IBM PC as the standard in the early 1980s. In the initial stages there were many competing architectures for the personal computer, and the emergence of the IBM version was brought about essentially by (unequal) competition. There was never any key decision taken by standards bodies or non-market groups to adopt the IBM version. A similar case, albeit with greater and more extended competition, was that concerning video formats: VHS, Betamax and V-2000 (see Gabel, 1991, ch. 3).

Agreement by adoption of a neutral standard occurs where, for a variety of reasons, no single approach has become dominant and there is some degree of consensus on the need to ensure compatibility through an additional standard—in the sense of a consistent and predictable expectation. This is in part exemplified by the OSI model in the field of telecommunications, and the work on data storage (i.e. IRDS) in information management. In both cases, however, the situation is not entirely harmonious, and as a consequence the story is not yet complete. The ubiquitousness of the RS232 interface is perhaps one of the few successful neutral standards in IS/IT.

The third mechanism, adoption of gateways, occurs where existing practices or products are well established, there is no prospect of one dominant form emerging, and the costs of transition outweigh the benefits of compatibility and interconnection. In such instances new products will appear which serve as gateways across otherwise incompatible ranges. The obvious everyday example would be connectors across 110 V and 220 V supplies. (Although even these standards are not quite consistent themselves, e.g. with the 220 V sometimes being 200 or 240 V.) Here the costs of an additional component are far less than the costs of changing existing configurations.

Gabel's entire argument is couched in terms of the economics of achieving compatibility. He uses the term *network* to define 'groups of products which have been designed to go together by a common reference to a design standard' (1991, p. 3). A network could then be a range of products from one specific supplier, or extend to all products or components based around a common feature.

Compatibility can then be achieved within a single network as well as across networks. Ensuring and maintaining such compatibility is not cost free; on the other hand, neither is it benefit free. The problem, however, is that sometimes those bearing the costs will not reap much of the benefit; and others, who Gabel terms *free-loaders*, will benefit but at no cost to themselves.

Gabel distinguishes between two dimensions of compatibility, both particularly relevant to IS. *Multi-vendor compatibility* concerns access across products from different suppliers. This may be achieved directly, e.g. in telecommunications equipment, and here the compatibility refers to the equipment itself, and is designed to produce an enhanced 'product': this could be identified by the term *interoperability*. On the other hand, there may be indirect compatibility via a *complementary product*, e.g. different brands of film camera via 35 mm film, or different brands of VHS machines via VHS cassette. Here the compatibility refers to the ability for the same function to be carried out by different products using the same item: this could be termed *interchange*.

Multi-vintage compatibility refers to compatibility found in ranges of products from a single supplier, e.g. new releases of products being compatible with earlier ones, or having a common set of complementary products. Computer peripherals are often examples of the former, and mainframe operating systems of the latter. The multi-vintage form is important because it can often be a consideration preventing adoption of the multi-vendor type, since a move to the latter may well result in the products of a supplier failing to be compatible with its own earlier product range(s). To use the example of operating systems again, many suppliers were keen to adopt UNIX in some form, but were prevented from doing so since they would have been unable to provide an upgrade to UNIX from their proprietary operating systems.

The concern with upgrades introduces a further point made by Gabel: that compatibility is often a matter of degree. Thus to say two products are compatible, one must further define the degree of functionality this encompasses. Many printers are sold as compatible with specific software and hardware, but this does not mean that all the facilities of each can be utilized. (I speak, as I suspect do many, from bitter and frustrating experience.) A basic form of compatibility may be cheap and easy to achieve; more extensive kinds will be expensive and may preclude other benefits.

The conclusion as far as Gabel is concerned is that compatibility is a common good in itself, but it will not arrive without cost. It is, therefore, important to locate those with most to gain from compatibility, or most to lose from its continuing absence. They must become at least in part the providers of the necessary resources to promote and sustain compatibility. But here the competition between the three different mechanisms identified earlier is evident. Although it may be obvious to alight on the development of public domain standards as the sole solution to problems caused by non-compatibility, in most cases adhering to such a standard would necessitate transfer from one (proprietary) network to another: the 'neutral' one effected by establishing the standard. Yet such transfer will by definition impose costs, since it will differ from any of the pre-existing networks. The benefits will tend to accrue to suppliers, permitting all of them to address wider sections of the market than were available through their own branded networks. The larger suppliers may have less to gain, particularly if their own vendor-specific network is extensive and well established: hence IBM's notorious reputation as spoiler or rival in the development of standards, now somewhat abated as their market-share has declined.

Small or specialist suppliers should have a great deal to gain, since they will be able to reach considerably larger numbers of consumers; but on the other hand, some of these smaller companies may have thrived precisely because there was no neutral standard, and they could supply gateway-type services and components that bridged otherwise incompatible technologies.

This should mean that certain small companies will readily involve themselves in 'neutral' standards making, while larger organizations will be more reluctant to do so. This is not always the case, and anyway there is no clear demarcation between large and small. In the computing field, until recently, everyone was small in comparison with IBM, although in a rapidly expanding market this was not particularly problematic since each vendor's specific network or customer base was growing. It was only when growth was no longer a certainty that the non-IBM organizations saw that it was in their mutual interests to bear the costs of producing and evolving to neutral standards to rival IBM's dominance: hence, for example, the OSI standardization initiatives.

For customers, the existence of a neutral standard ought to be of benefit, provided it is well established and fairly widely adhered to by a proportion of the suppliers. It may even be possible for such a standard to coexist with proprietary products. Again IBM provides an example of such coexistence. IBM's EBCDIC standard for character representation continued in existence for many years despite the appearance of the US standard ASCII representation. This situation of dual networks was an improvement on the numerous forms of representation that had existed before widespread adoption of ASCII, but it was still irksome since it prevented full interchange of items such as computer magnetic tape and software. A variety of bridging technologies became available, and eventually some became 'standard' components of most mainframe machines. The arrival of the PC finally confirmed the ASCII format, and EBCDIC is now of limited interest except as a historical quirk.

ACHIEVING COMPATIBILITY

However, compatibility can be achieved and assured, the chief benefit for customers is that they can plan their purchasing and development strategies with some assurance that they will not have to endure the costs and upheavals of obsolescence and wholesale replacement which result from finding that their earlier strategies have left them with systems that cannot be upgraded or enhanced. It would appear, therefore, that customers would find it in their own collective interests to combine to develop and enforce neutral standards, as this would give them independence from particular suppliers or cartels. But again the situation is not quite as simple.

First it assumes that a significant group of customers have similar interests, and can combine to agree on what the neutral standard should address. Secondly, and more crucially, it assumes that customers can bear the costs of standardization and find this preferable to accepting the outcome of Gabel's network competition source of compatibility. This is not a cost-free form of compatibility—the main initial cost is often borne by those who had earlier bought alternative technologies—but it appears not to involve any expense other than the costs of purchasing the technology itself. Thus Windows provides an example of compatibility developing through network competition, but it is brought about at the expense of lock-in to a specific supplier via a proprietary standard. This is not the same as occurred with the IBM PC, since in the latter case the standard was open to the market and IBM did not levy a price or rent on the architecture. In the case of Windows, Microsoft charge a rent for the software, and restrict access to their product. IBM did try a similar strategy with PS/2, but by then they were no longer the dominant player in the market.

If consumer interests did ever consolidate sufficiently to enforce a *de jure* Windows standard, this would involve removing the ownership from Microsoft and finding resources to develop and probably extend the standard. Although there may be arguments in favour of this course of action, they would need to counter the apparent cost-free nature of the current position. In any event it is unlikely that Windows users form a coherent group capable of such consolidation; although the user base is large enough for a segment of the market to break away and enforce their own specific demands and products. (This is especially true of those Windows *users* who are in fact suppliers of Windows-based products: they may well have sufficient interest and weight to force the development of a *de jure* standard.)

All these complications and qualifications are evidence of the complexities of developing standardization and compatibility in IT. Suppliers may seek to prevent standardization of some aspects where they hold some dominance, and yet actively seek it in other areas where they perceive market opportunities currently denied them. Customers, who theoretically ought to have a common interest in enhancing compatibility, are for the most part too dispersed and diverse to achieve this; and furthermore are unwilling or unable to provide the resources to develop and enforce the standards: they all prefer to be free-loaders.

As a result, all too often the development of neutral, public domain standards is a measure of last resort—albeit one with a lengthy gestation period. The costs of developing the standard were often met from government sources, but this is increasingly less common. The greatest costs are borne by customers who have purchased incompatible technologies, and overpriced services and products; but it is difficult to use this as a justification for obtaining resources and financing for developing the *de jure* standards in the first place. This is partly because the benefits will only accrue after the standard is in place, and often to a more limited degree than if the standard had been in place earlier. Furthermore the benefits will be far more diffuse, and those who have provided the resources will not necessarily feel that the benefit matches the cost. This situation is as much a fault of the customers as it is of the suppliers and standards makers. In a rapidly changing field such as IS/IT, it is a critical matter, but it is unclear how this can be ameliorated.

Gabel (1991) provides an excellent discussion of the character of standardization, and he illustrates his work with some interesting and apposite examples. The main point to be noted in this context is that the search for compatibility must be seen within the market context of competition and costs weighed against benefits; and that formal, public-domain standards are only one aspect of this.

INFLUENCING STANDARDIZATION

Whatever the mechanisms that result in a demand for standardization, and even if there is a critical mass behind a base technology at any one time, the extent to which these can produce and sustain a standard and act as a foundation for control and management may be severely limited. Organizations may still have to decide whether they simply follow the lead of significant others, risk branching out on their own to some extent, or add their representation to bodies of like-minded organizations intent on influencing the development of standards in some form or other.

This last approach will almost certainly involve some contribution to standardization in the public domain, even if it means attempting to promote a proprietary standard to a public one, e.g. establishing or joining a particular user group. But locating the best forum for this activity may be problematic. Many of the public bodies charged with development and progression of standards are too often dominated by professional standards makers, who are so imbued with the intricacies and stratagems of standards development that they no longer see standards as a means to an end, but as ends in themselves. This often results in arcane standards, and in deliberations that preclude many of the interests which should be involved in standards work.

The alternatives may include less formal bodies, perhaps user groups or those representing the interests of specific market segments. The user group bodies may serve some purpose, but often they are curtailed by the supplier or by dominant user organizations. For these reasons, user groups tend to be less amenable to the very widest considerations for standards, but on the other hand the issues at the centre of their attention will be derived from clear concerns located within a specific domain, and resolution of such issues will directly serve those who promulgate the standards. This will counteract the tendency to feel that standards emerge only to serve very general interests, at great cost and little specific or eventual benefit to participating organizations—all too often with the main beneficiaries being the standards makers rather than the potential standards users.

This should not be taken as a criticism specific to standards making in the IS area. In fact these observations and reproaches of standards makers and standards forums apply to all domains in which standards are an issue. In the IS domain, however, these weaknesses are exacerbated since the area is comparatively new, developing at enormous speed, and with relatively little agreement on even central issues—hence even the emergence of consensus at a core level is arduous and severely constrained. It is not too surprising that the safety-in-numbers criterion offered by standardization through proprietary products appears attractive, even if it has limitations. No one ever got fired for buying IBM in the 1970s; but what is the equivalent for the 1990s?

The advent of the PC has promoted standardization, since the technology is no longer restricted to those involved with mainframe machines. But it has also expanded the use and extent of the technology, and this increase, in both numerical terms and range of application, necessitates standardization. The 1980s and 1990s have, therefore, seen the advent of standardization initiatives at the levels of basic hardware, operating systems, and communications. There is even agreement on a fairly extensive vocabulary and conceptual basis for IT and associated areas. Different suppliers can now be relied upon to use the same terminology, namely that used in standards in the area of IT and communications, i.e. the OSI model, interface standards, etc.

DIFFICULTIES IN STANDARDIZING IS AND SE—CONCEPTUAL AND ORGANIZATIONAL

In the less concrete aspects of IS, however, standards development is far less advanced; it is even more fraught with complications, and is certainly no less critical. These less evident aspects may not be as dependent on the intricacies of the specific technologies, but this intangibility makes them harder to standardize, particularly since there is often no agreement on their central features and characteristics. Even an agreement on basic terminology and vocabulary has proved problematic. Thus attempts to standardize aspects of the development process, analysis and design methods, testing and assessment approaches, and so on are inevitably severely hampered by the absence of any essential or profound agreement on the nature of the particular topic itself. Many texts and specifications have to start almost from first principles and define key concepts—the present text is no exception to this. To use (correctly) some currently favoured terminology: there is no established IS paradigm.

It might be countered that there is no reason to standardize these aspects of IS. It is only necessary to standardize the fundamental technological products in order to ensure compatibility. This is to misunderstand the relationship between compatibility and standards as the discussion of Gabel's ideas has already illustrated. It is also to misconceive the role that standards might play in IS concerns. In addition it is to exhibit an indifference to the major proportion of cost and source of risk in the development of IS—exactly those non-technological aspects. These issues will be dealt with below, but first some attention must be given to the confusion surrounding the concepts of the IS domain.

Even the use of the term 'information systems' is problematic. In the UK the main forum for IS/IT standards is the BSI. Within its structure there is one main section concerned with *Delivering Information Systems to Customers* (DISC). The primary objective of this subgroup is 'to help enterprises improve their operational effectiveness by accelerating standardization in information systems and by promoting standards and making them easier to exploit'.

The technical work programmes are carried out by technical committees, grouped into four areas as follows:

- Information Systems Technology (IST)
- Advanced Manufacturing Technology (AMT)
- Information and Documentation (DOT)
- Telecommunications (TCT)

The focus of IST is based on satisfying the demands to integrate and exploit the full range of IS/IT products and services. The specific areas of concern include the following:

- Interoperability—networks, OSI, messaging, etc.
- Software engineering
- Application portability
- User interfaces
- Systems security and reliability
- Databases

Unfortunately the structure of the BSI has not managed to keep abreast of the rapid advances and changes in the IS area, and so many of the committees and terms of reference are somewhat outdated. This is not a reflection on the BSI, more an effect of the rapid changes in technology. There are a large number of technical committees within the IST area, and one of them, IST/15, is the one responsible for 'Software Engineering'. (Until comparatively recently it was called 'Software Development and Systems Documentation'.) As one of its key tasks, this committee has the responsibility of contributing towards and shadowing the activities of the equivalent ISO grouping, SC7 Software Engineering.

Both the UK and the international groups are plagued with uncertainty regarding their breadth and depth of responsibility. Software engineering is a comparatively new field, and one of extensive innovation and expansion. It is not surprising, therefore, that some proportion of effort has been, and continues to be, expended on defining and characterizing the area itself. Some might suggest that perhaps too much effort has been applied to this; furthermore they would point out that all too often the results of such work fail to clarify or resolve demarcation or other issues, and simply add to the confusion.

At present there is at least some agreement on the concept of *software engineering*. There is no standard definition, but a working definition can be found in one of the key texts in the field: 'The establishment and use of sound engineering principles in order to obtain economically, software that is reliable and works efficiently on real machines' (Pressman, 1992, p. 23). There is, however, less unanimity on the full scope of software engineering. This is in part due to the expansion of the capability of the technology itself, and its applications and uses, which have developed and changed qualitatively as well as quantitatively.

It is not the straightforward increase in the number of computers, but rather the scope of activities in which they play a role that is critical. This has led to the recognition of concerns which originate and emanate well beyond the confines of the hardware and software. It has even led to a profound questioning of the ramifications of 'engineering' when appended to the term 'software' (see Bryant, 1989). Hence a recent text on software engineering concludes its opening chapter: 'Software engineering is defined not as a branch of engineering, but rather as a discipline whose aim is the production of quality software that satisfies user's [*sic*] needs, and is delivered on time and within budget' (Schach, 1993, p. 17). Taken to its logical conclusion, particularly in correctly positioning the apostrophe in *users'*, leads to accepting a plurality of different users, and hence to the full scope of IS concerns rather than software engineering concerns. This broadening of scope is critical, and leads to an extension of the role of standards.

Following this trend, some recent publications have begun to dispense with the term 'software engineering' altogether, offering alternatives such as 'computer-based systems engineering', or 'engineering of computer-based systems', or 'software-based systems'. Others retain 'software engineering', but only as a specialism within the wider realm of 'systems engineering' (see, for instance, the issue of *IEEE Software*, March 1994, on requirements engineering).

Whereas the initial meaning of the term 'software engineering' may have been not much more than a sophisticated synonym for program construction, incorporating best engineering practice (c.1968), it now conveys far more, embodying aspects such as the management of large-scale software development, requirements capture, validation against customer and client requirements, verification, testing, and formal certification of software systems in operation (see Bryant, 1989).

This expansion is best illustrated by the transformation in one of the standard texts for the subject: Ian Sommerville's *Software Engineering*. Its first and second editions were fairly condensed volumes of around 200 pages, mainly concerned with program design and testing. The second edition appeared in 1984 and was the main recommended text for relevant courses in the UK. By 1989 the third edition appeared, now more than 600 pages in length, and with a far more extensive scope. The fourth edition—an update of the previous edition—appeared with almost indecent haste in 1992; 31 chapters and 600+ pages. In this latest edition Sommerville does not produce a specific definition of software engineering, but instead offers a section outlining a whole host of issues critical to software development, including 'technical' factors such as reliability, maintainability, and so on; and 'non-technical' ones such as communication and group working. A similar set of observations applies to the equivalent US text by Roger Pressman (1992).

Moreover many 1990s' definitions of software engineering now explicitly refer to information systems, e.g. 'software engineering is the systematic application of scientific and technical knowledge, methods, and experience to the design, implementation and testing of software and its documentation to optimize information systems procedures and support' (ISO/IEC *Information Technology—Vocabulary* DIS 2382-1, 01.04.040). The assumption seems to be that the only viable constraint upon the domain of software engineering is the absence of any software: if software is involved, so too will be the concerns of software engineering. But this should not be taken to imply that all or even most issues within such 'software-based systems' are concerned with the software itself. This is precisely the point at which IS issues develop beyond those of software engineering. The IS realm is increasingly marked by the ubiquitousness of software; but it is a necessary though not sufficient component of any IS.

This ambiguity between software engineering and IS issues is well grounded in organizational reality, and there is extensive understanding of the interaction among practitioners and researchers as evidenced by the growing literature, specialist groups and conferences, professional and vocational courses, and so on. Unfortunately the standards world has not yet mirrored this development and change of focus. This is hardly surprising. The software engineering focus is relatively new, but the IS focus is even more novel, and there is little agreement on what IS issues entail.

In addition to these conceptual problems, as far as standards organizations are concerned, there is also an element of inertia to overcome in changing any existing structure—particularly an international one based around consensus. This is further complicated, since the emergence of an ISO body concerned with IS issues would not simply develop from the software engineering group, but would also have to draw upon other bodies such as those concerned with user issues, systems design, and so on. This involves cutting across collective and personal fiefdoms.

A start on developing an arena for discussion of IS standards issues has been made at the level of the European Union, where the standards activities are in a much less advanced and hence more fluid stage. Thus rather than creating an EU version of SC7 (Software Engineering), a committee has been established specifically with the remit of information systems engineering. This is partly due to the fact that the EU standards body, CEN, has only come into existence comparatively recently: IS have more currency in the 1990s than software engineering.

It remains to be seen how the IS body develops, and what ramifications its activities will have at national and international levels. At present the position is marked by a fair degree of confusion. There is agreement on the scope of the committee, with ISE defined as 'the systematic, disciplined application of knowledge, methods, and experience to the provision and support of IS, bridging strategic goals/requirements and operational tools'. But there is not yet agreement on what is meant by the use of the term IS in that definition. (NB: the term 'bridging' is ambiguous, and should be understood more as 'encompassing'.)

INFORMATION SYSTEMS—A DEFINITION AND DISCUSSION

Clearly a key issue in seeking to develop strategies in the domain of IS, and IS standards, is the scope and nature of the term 'information system' itself. Current literature shows a marked reluctance to offer definitions of IS—yet the term is ubiquitous, and often confusingly used synonymously with software system or IT. The reluctance is in part understandable, since the only safe thing that can be said is that 'IS is *more* than IT', i.e. the system is more than the embodiment of the operating technology—hardware, software, communications, etc. (see Fig. 2.1). What this 'more' actually is, and how it differs from and is related to the technology itself are the key questions begged by this statement.

Many sources which might be referred to for a definition of IS either use the term without defining it, or simply define it in terms of another term: 'information technology' and 'software engineering' are the most common. This failure to clarify the term merely adds to the confusion engendered in

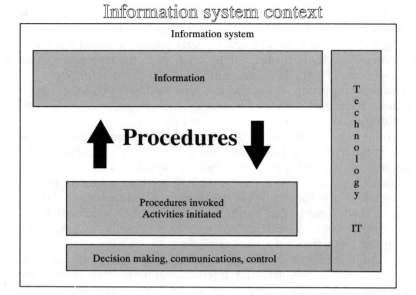

Figure 2.1 Information systems engineering and software engineering.

the minds of specialists and non-specialists alike when IS-related topics are discussed.

For the purposes of this discussion the following definition is offered:

> An information system (IS) can be defined as a system whose objective and functions encompass the gathering, accepting, processing, storing, retrieving, producing and presenting of information. This provision must be relevant to a context, in such a way that the information is accessible and useful to those who wish to use it, including managers, staff, clients, and other interested stakeholders.

In essence an IS is a human activity system which may or may not involve the use of computers and other technology: increasingly it will do so. The functions of an IS are enacted by differing combinations of people and devices—the latter increasingly and predominantly based around information and communications technology (IT). The information which is the object of these activities must be of persisting relevance within the (organizational) context within which the IS operates.

The scope of IS-related activities extends significantly further than the technology that supports some of its key functions. These additional aspects concern the interactional, social, and organizational facets of the system. These aspects cannot be encompassed in purely technological terms, but some of them can be evoked by applying systems concepts to the understanding of information *systems*.

An IS must be seen as:

- *A set of components which interact* This implies a need for central planning, control, and coordination. It also introduces the concepts of hierarchy and emergence, i.e. some components are composed of other components, and they relate in a hierarchical fashion, with properties of the higher levels emerging only at those levels, and not being reducible to the characteristics or properties of the component parts.
- *Having a boundary and scope* It may be difficult to reach agreement on where a particular IS begins or ends, but the relationship of the IS with other systems and the overall organizational (business) system must be addressed.
- *Being goal-seeking and goal-supporting* An IS must be coupled to contextual or organizational goals, but must also have its own IS-specific objectives. The goals themselves will in part be imposed by the contextual system—'the super-system'; others will be derived from the nature of the IS itself. The nature of those objectives, and their relative priorities, is a strategic issue. Decisions relating to alternative means of achieving the goals are tactical and operational issues.
- *Requiring coordination and design of input and output* An IS does not exist in isolation; its operation and effectiveness is not merely a matter of internal refinement, but is critically dependent upon its contextual integration with other systems, its super-system, and its environment.
- *Having a tendency towards increasing entropy* An IS requires management and control, and must be seen as inherently precarious and changeable; otherwise it is in danger of becoming obsolete.

All this implies that the information processing requirement at the heart of an IS is a persisting activity, which must be sensitive to change, and may be critical to an organization's success or even survival.

IS functions are both controlled and controlling: they help to control organization decision-making, but must also receive feedback from those activities. It must also be recognized that there may be many ways of reaching the organizational or IS-specific goals, and that a business driven approach is preferable to a technology-driven one.

THE DOMAIN OF IS—ENGINEERING OR MANAGEMENT?

Even if there is no widespread agreement on details, the domain of IS is now recognized as authentic, with specific aspects and features, issues and concerns. These emerge in part from the combination of facets—technical, interactional, and social—which contribute to the development and operation of an information system.

The influence of the software aspect, and technical ones in general, has led to the use of the term *information systems engineering* (ISE) to apply to the practices involved. This is somewhat misleading given the narrow sense in which engineering can be and has been understood. It does, however, point to the sorts of consideration which are at least part of the central core of the area: ISE is the systematic, disciplined application of knowledge, methods, and experience to the provision and support of IS, encompassing strategic objectives and operational tools.

Another term used in this domain is *information management* (IM), defined as 'the approach or policy which an organization adopts to manage its data/information resource' (Hirschheim quoted in Boaden and Lockett, 1991). Others have used the term *information resource management* (IRM) in similar fashion, although Lee uses it to define the pinnacle of a three-stage development beginning with electronic data processing (EDP), progressing to management information systems (MIS), and then to IRM (quoted in Boaden and Lockett, 1991).

The relationship between IS, IT, and IM can be visualized from Fig. 2.2. This indicates that the technology supports the functioning of disparate information systems, which themselves form components of the overall IS

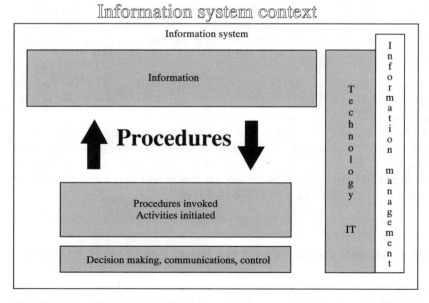

Figure 2.2 Information systems, information technology, and information management in the IS context.

for an organization. The control of the individual systems and supporting technology is the concern of IM. (The term information system management, ISM, is practically synonymous with IM, but emphasizes the systems aspect of the resource.)

The importance of concepts such as ISE or IM is that they point to a range of issues extending well beyond technical and performance concerns of the system itself. As a way of avoiding terminological confusion, rather than seeking a definitive vocabulary, for the purposes of this discussion IM will be seen as a component of ISE. The domain of IS is then the topic for ISE practices and expertise.

This extended range of IS issues, centring around ISE and IM, indicates the role standards need to play in enhancing interchange and interoperability as well as convenience, ease of use, interconnectability, safety, risk reduction, integration of technological improvement, and so on. This is particularly relevant given the amount of resources organizations already invest in their information systems—a sum that is certain to grow.

Any attempts to develop IS standards must recognize the full range of IS characteristics. In addition it must be seen that IS/ISE issues are far more complex than many (most) other 'engineering' specialties. This complexity is partly a result of IS/ISE encompassing software development. As Brooks noted in a seminal article, software entities are 'more complex for their size than perhaps any other human construct' (Brooks, 1986). But the IS realm is further complicated by aspects such as planning, management, control, and a focus and resource for social and organizational interaction: complexity on top of complexity.

In addition the IS itself has to provide a sustained service, satisfying the demands of a wide range of users—or a significant subset thereof. The service, however, can only be provided once the system, or a significant component, is in place. This is no trivial matter, and hence the development process itself must be a topic for analysis and assessment, as well as a crucial site for standardization activities, since planning, predictability and control are demanded. This has resulted in a concentration on the IS development process, but should not obscure the primacy of service provision to users of the actual system (see Chapter 4). Any attempt to understand the emergence of specific ISE issues and standardization strategies can only be understood against this context of process and service.

Since IS service provision is intimately linked with that of other service provision, and with administration and bureaucracy in general, the influence of public sector interests is a key component. This is the case even where the official public sector is relatively small; it will anyway still be large when compared with any single private organization, and in addition there will tend to be a quasi-public sector. Given that by current reckoning at least 3 per cent of GDP is directly linked to the IS area, anything which improves delivery and operation of IS ought to make a significant contribution to domestic economies and public sector performance.

BARRIERS TO PROGRESS AND INDICATORS FOR OVERCOMING THEM

Any programme that has a realistic chance of engendering better, or best, practice in IS provision and support ought to be welcome and encouraged. Thus there should be an easy alliance between large organizations with significant investment and reliance on IS service provision and public sector bodies. Both should be keen to promote an environment in which planning and development are supported by planning frameworks and criteria for assessment and comparison of products and services, as well as by the widest possible bases for selection and compatibility. Such an impressive combination of interested parties ought to be able to resource such activities and ensure the satisfaction of such objectives. Yet there is little evidence that any such alliances are developing, nor even any appreciation that such combinations are necessary and likely to prove effective.

One reason for this failure is that it cannot be assumed that standards-making activities are recognized as a way of promoting such issues and resolving the problems. There is growing scepticism concerning the efficacy of standards even in the relatively constrained areas of technological integration. The OSI approach, while warmly welcomed in its early stages, does not appear to have resolved many of the issues relevant to user organizations. This has led to a growing credibility gap, particularly outside supplier-led consortia, regarding the ability of standards to deliver *openness* and compatibility.

Studies such as the *SMARTIE* (1992) project indicate that many 'standards' relevant to software development are not fit for the purpose. In the terms of various EU directives, they are 'technically inadequate or the means to establish conformity is lacking'. To use the terms introduced by Gabel (1991), the standards that do exist in the area of software development have not resolved the issue of incompatibility across competing networks, they do not offer a neutral alternative nor do they provide the basis for meaningful comparison of the products and processes emanating from competing sources.

This situation is exacerbated since many of the issues critical to IS improvement programmes are dispersed across numerous bodies and organizations. Issues and the standards that might resolve them are not integrated. If the range of issues cannot be reconciled, and the efforts of the relevant bodies consolidated, further progress will be thwarted. Even if this position can be ameliorated, the many levels of supplier interest—with their own network—will act against pressures to standardize. To return to the

Economist article cited in the previous chapter: 'Every firm wants a monopoly—and every firm wants to call it an open standard', i.e. every supplier wants its network of offerings to win the battle for compatibility via network competition.

More positively there are indications that interests are beginning to coalesce around the idea of a more constrained and user-led perspective of IS practices and issues. This means that standards cannot be supplier-based or product-based, effectively precluding significant sections of the user-base. Consideration has to be given to consumer-oriented and issue-based perspectives. The most generally recognized issue is that IS must afford enhanced business support through better ISE practices. This perspective has come to the fore in part as a result of the necessity for wider funding of standards initiatives, although in many instances it has not yet been translated into detailed and manageable work programmes. The small coteries of standards makers have had to expand to encompass wider ranges of interests, and more diverse participants. This is to be welcomed, particularly if it results in clear declarations concerning standards as means to other ends, rather than as ends in themselves.

In the development and provision of IS, the facility to summon the interests and skills embodying these diversified perspectives and best practices is dependent in part upon recognized definitions of IS/ISE phases and the interfaces between them. Furthermore there must be some guide that relates IS activities and imperatives to each other, and to contextual and user demands. This is slightly paradoxical, since it means that a standard view of the IS terrain and development process must form a component of the basis that will attract groups to participate in standards making for IS. In other words, standards must provide the fundamentals for further work on standards.

This paradox emanates from the disparities between people's views of the character and nature of the IS domain. This results in the present situation where there has been some broad agreement on the necessity for standard models of IS, but a plethora of contending candidate 'frameworks' and definitions. This has produced a good deal of acrimony between the champions of particular frameworks, and enlarged the camp of sceptics who consider such efforts wasteful and ultimately doomed to failure.

Much of the initial work done in this area has concentrated on the software components. The Standardization Framework for Software Engineering and the IEEE Master Plan for Software Engineering Standards are two examples (JTC1, 1992; IEEE, 1993). The Reference Model for IS Development (Heym and Osterl, 1991) uses the wider IS perspective, and the Euromethod project is due to offer a taxonomy of required standards to support ISE.

Two of the SC7 Software Engineering working groups are developing standards in the areas of lifecycle processes and lifecycle management.

Unfortunately there are some demarcation problems between the groups, and a certain level of disagreement on even fundamental issues within the groups. If no clear resolution is in sight perhaps the standards makers will need to adopt a pragmatic and shorter-term view of IS, leaving it to others to proffer models of the domain as research products which may then stand the test of application and use by IS professionals. A post-modern context of pluralism and peaceful coexistence seems more sensible than any single dogma at present.

The above at least gives a flavour of the sorts of activities and issues pertinent to ISE. Rather than extend the discussion to cover the minutiae of standards-making bodies, it is more important to consider certain key aspects of IS/IT from the perspective of those with direct relevant experience and a practical slant on the issues. One such authority is Carl Cargill, writing as an employee of DEC, but with a keen grasp of many of the issues around IT standardization.

CARGILL'S VIEW OF IT STANDARDS—80 PER CENT PERSPIRATION; 20 PER CENT INSPIRATION

For Cargill 'a standard is the deliberate acceptance by a group of people having common interests or background of a *quantifiable metric* that influences their behaviour and activities by permitting a common interchange' (Cargill, 1989, p. 13, my italics). This is a somewhat different conception from that expressed in BS0 (in Chapter 1), although it is to a large degree compatible with the BSI perspective.

The most noticeable distinctions are as follows:

1. That consensus is replaced by the more limited and direct concept of a like-minded group of people.
2. The standard is manifest in the form of a quantifiable metric rather than the more equivocal yet versatile notion of a set of rules, guidelines, procedures.
3. The objective of overall community benefit is absent; instead the aim of a common interchange is seen as an end in itself.

These distinctions can in part be explained by the position from which Cargill derives his ideas. He is writing from the American context, and within that is positioned within a specific company (DEC) within the IT realm. His work is, however, a key text with regard to IT standards, and his observations also have relevance to the IS domain in general.

Cargill regards IS/IT standardization as deficient, and is candid in his accusations and identification of culprits. Essentially he writes to warn people away from the misapprehension that standards provide easy solutions to complex problems. The temptation of those seeking order and certainty in situations of flux and chaos is to 'rush to standards'. This is based on flawed reasoning, and owes a good deal to the paucity of substance and insight emanating from those regarded as standards experts and authorities. Thus he notes that most of the texts on standards focus on one specific standard, and then offer general conclusions and lessons for all standards-making activities. (In case the present text seems an example of this, it should be noted that although the SSADM standard forms the focus for the second part of the discussion, the first part is drawn from a wide variety of sources and experiences in standards making and not merely from a single focus. Ultimately the reader must decide if this claim for wider relevance is justified.)

In general the standards bodies and the academic community demonstrate a poor understanding of the nature of standards and the processes involved in their development. Cargill seeks to remedy this deficiency, and attempts to develop an explanatory framework that encompasses different types of standard and a wide variety of activities contributing to standards making.

He first introduces the distinction between voluntary and regulatory standards. The former are seen as more appropriate to 'volatile areas with competing technological and application solutions available, where there are intense user and provider dynamics' (p. 22). Regulatory standards 'are more useful when there is only a single acceptable solution to a problem' (p. 22). Their purpose is to regulate activity rather than to encourage development and growth.

The objectives of the standards makers, in terms of benefits accruing, are the same in both cases: 'interchangeability, convenience, ease of use, interconnectability, safety, risk reduction, integration of technological improvement, and so on' (p. 22).

Clearly it cannot be correct to cluster all these aspects together as relevant to all standards making. Cargill seems to conflate the idea of standards as a basis for compatibility, *consistent and predictable expectation*, with that of standards as a basis for assessment, *qualitative comparison*. But the features listed are fairly comprehensive, and provide a useful input to any exercise for deciding priorities for any specific standards-making project. If none of the benefits listed by Cargill will accrue, then perhaps the standard is not worth developing.

In deciding upon a standardization strategy there could even be discussion of whether or not a voluntary or regulatory standard would prove most suitable. In resolving this, matters such as the necessity to consider enforcement and render compulsion have to be considered. In reality, however, the choice between voluntary or regulatory will mostly be dictated by external factors such as the market pressures which inform

Gabel's argument, and 'public interest' arguments which emanate from regulatory bodies.

Cargill considers that voluntary standards derive their strength from being market driven and attracting industry support. Those initiating and developing such standards need to be skilled and imaginative in understanding how to integrate user needs with industry innovation. Such standards will tend to be difficult to produce since they will rely entirely upon achieving consensus, often from an initially conflict-ridden basis. Furthermore, since any final standard will be voluntary, there will be no mechanisms for encouraging compliance and guaranteeing enforcement. However, should a highly visible or influential supplier or consumer organization lend obvious support to such a standard, it will encourage others to do likewise.

Regulatory standards, on the other hand, are far easier to control and develop since they will emerge from a centralized process, specifying adherence and compliance, and accompanied by reward and penalty structures. This is a source of both strength and weakness. In order to operate as regulatory standards such documents will have to be detailed and precisely written. Once in place they will be awkward to change, and this inflexibility may render them obsolete in a rapidly changing environment. If they do remain in force for any length of time, litigation will develop as contending parties seek to clarify the exact meaning and extent of the standard. Since the application of the standard will be mandatory in many cases, there may be hostility to its use and any associated enforcement agency.

As will be seen in the later detailed sections concerned with the standard for SSADM, the distinction between voluntary and regulatory types of standard does not always apply as a clear division. But the distinction has merit as the extremes in a range of possibilities, varying from completely voluntary at one extreme, gradually becoming less consensus-based, and finally becoming mandatory at the other. This supports the position explained in Chapter 1, that standards exist to facilitate negotiations between contractual parties. Even for mandatory standards the parties will themselves select and operate specific standards as a basis for achieving agreement.

In fact Cargill recognizes that the distinction is not a simple one, and that the importance of standards will vary across different domains. What will apply to all motivations for standards making, however, will be the market-driven demand for some or all of the benefits listed previously. This echoes many of the points made by Gabel. On the basis of his analysis of standards, what concerns Cargill is that although there is now general acceptance of the benefits of standards, and recognition of the market-balancing purpose they serve, standards-making bodies have failed to evolve to capture these strengths and harness them to achieving the objective of developing relevant and necessary standards.

THREE DIMENSIONS OF STANDARDS

In the 'IT realm', characterized by uncertainty and rapid change, Cargill stresses that voluntary standards must for the present predominate. These 'consensus' standards vary in terms of three dimensions:

- *Importance*—their importance to the relevant domain.
- *Implementation or conceptual standard*—whether they apply to an implementation (for a specific device) as opposed to a set of concepts.
- *Process or product standard*—the procedure for construction is the target of the standard, as opposed to the outcome of the procedure.

The dimension of importance focuses on the views both customers and suppliers have regarding the need for a standard. Customers will demand standards to ensure compatibility, better use of resources, reduced costs, and a mechanism to exert pressure on suppliers to provide reliable and predictable products and services. This is one way to persuade consumers that standards are important, and that their development and application should be resourced effectively.

Suppliers, on the other hand, will either see standards as having a negative impact on future developments, or on the contrary will recognize that standards in many cases will grant them access to specific technologies and allow them a firmer basis for innovation and product enhancement. Gabel's points about network economies, limitations, and opportunities are another way of expressing this.

All of these perspectives, with their concomitant motivations and reservations, must be taken into account in seeking to develop standards. Yet all too often the 'importance' attributed to the identified need for a standard is the result of lack of planning on the part of suppliers and/or consumers, or the dawning of the realization that some regulatory mechanism is lacking, and some measure of control must be effected— leading to a rush to standards. Thus all too often standards are seen as a substitute for effective management, control, and planning. If standards are developed on this basis, they will fail completely or at best be short lived, since by the time they are in place further problems will beset the domain and it is extremely unlikely that the standard will retain its relevance.

Achieving consensus for voluntary standards must be undertaken with the assumption that such agreement will be 'predictive and future oriented' (Cargill, 1989 p. 28), and not an attempt to solve an immediate problem.

> A standard . . . can be envisaged as a plan that represents the proposed activities of the industry in dealing with an issue . . . a standard is the written solution to a future industry problem.   (pp. 28–9)

This is probably wildly optimistic and overstates the case for standards as a component of far-sighted planning rather than as crisis measures. On the other hand, it is certainly true that those involved in standards development should not draw their motivation from existing predicaments and current issues, unless they are convinced that the difficulties will continue in the future. Moreover they ought to have some basis for believing that 'their standard' will retain relevance and force beyond the time of its delivery, not merely at the point of its conception. It is here that the true expertise of standards makers is likely to have most advantageous effect.

In a realm as dynamic and changing as IT, standards cannot be expected to address the future in any meaningful way, since such knowledge of the future is not available. Anyone involved in IT standards in the early 1980s could not possibly have envisaged the extent of the changes resulting from the introduction of PC technology. On the other hand, given that some aspects of the technology have now evolved for more than a decade, it is possible to assess the future to a limited extent, and plan and standardize accordingly.

Standards can be developed to reinforce particular patterns or practices in an industry segment; similarly they can be devised to alter such aspects. There is no way of 'future-proofing' standards, just as there is no way of 'future-proofing' any strategy. This is not a reason to abstain from planning, simply to note that any plans must be made with change and flexibility in mind.

Stressing and extending his own dictum that 'standards should be planned', Cargill also warns of the standard that causes unplanned change. Upon the three categories of standard—those that reinforce, revise, or have ill-determined consequences—he imposes the distinction between implementation and conceptual standards. Implementation types will tend to reinforce existing aspects. Thus the PC example could be seen as an implementation standard, gaining strength from its constraining power in a previously chaotic domain.

Cargill offers another example, that of the COBOL standard, 'which changes so that COBOL remains responsive to the current and future needs of the industry' (p. 29). The standard has gone through many revisions and updates, but 'the solution it provides . . . does not change but rather evolves to meet the changing needs of those who demanded it in the first place' (p. 29). In other words, the standard acts as a constraint on advancement precisely because it offers a stable and conventional platform for software development. (The cynic might argue that COBOL exemplifies the fourth—omitted—category from Cargill's classification: a standard that causes unplanned stasis.)

PRODUCT AND PROCESS STANDARDS

In contrast to the *evolutionary* implementation standards, conceptual standards are *revolutionary* and tend to appear at the behest of a supplier or someone prepared to champion a specific innovation. The example of the IEEE 802.3 Ethernet standard is given by Cargill, and although some (e.g. advocates of certain ring configurations) might argue that the Ethernet concept was not as innovatory as it might have been, it illustrates the point about a standard for an array of associated and intricate technologies rather than one targeted at a specific and clear technical issue.

Since the physical technology is changing so quickly, attempts to develop implementation standards will increasingly fail the test of future or long-term applicability. Thus *product* standards will almost always produce standards that are short-lived, at best; at worst they will be obsolete even before they are completed. (Many current standardization activities related to PC architectures may well suffer this fate.)

If standards are to retain relevance despite technical innovations they must address the *processes* that IT products are designed to support. A process standard 'focuses on the transmutation of a customer need into a customer solution' (p. 33). But this is not to say that process standards will inevitably endure, since they will have to be valid and favoured statements of real needs, derived from a clear understanding of the context, issues, and solutions.

The work on developing lifecycle processes and management standards are examples of potential process standards. The difficulties in gaining international consensus for such standards is perhaps indicative of a lack of agreement on the context and issues surrounding such standardization activities.

In the realm of IS as a whole, as opposed to the narrower IT focus of Cargill's work, the distinction between product and process does not apply as unambiguously or readily. This is because IS 'products', other than the immediately tangible ones, are often themselves generic, embodying an extensive and extensible solution to a range of requirements. To an extent these products are tangible representations for the completion of a specific process or group of processes, e.g. a requirements specification.

The advantage of identifying such products is that it is easier to mandate and acknowledge delivery of completed products than it is to be assured in some other way of the satisfactory completion of a process. This applies particularly to complex, multi-faceted processes such as IS development methods, as will be shown in later chapters. The disadvantage of such an orientation is that the term 'product' becomes overused and loses meaning and relevance, thereby obscuring the importance of the processes that underlie the product itself.

CARGILL'S TYPOLOGY OF STANDARDS

Combining these dimensions of standards, Cargill argues that there are 'four possible valid combinations' (p. 35):

- Implementation/product
- Implementation/process
- Conceptual/product
- Conceptual/process.

The implementation/product combination is the most common for IT, particularly in areas where there is some stability. The PC standard is an example since it affirms and constrains existing and potential technical innovation. This is not to say that it prevents development, but equally it does channel or focus advancement within a particular framework. 'Although the market that uses this type of standard is dynamic, I believe it is safe to say that it has an aura of predictability' (p. 36). In this sense the implementation/product type of standard is a standard in the sense of a consistent and predictable expectation as described in Chapter 1.

The combination involved in the implementation/process type seems contradictory. The implementation part emanates from the present, the process part points to the future; but Cargill points out that increasingly requirements are either 'too complex or too simple to be met by a single product' (p. 36). In this case the standard must be aimed at defining the process for satisfying the need, rather than the product(s) that result in this accomplishment.

The general area of communications is replete with these sorts of issues, and the development of these sorts of standards. Some of Gabel's points about gateways and other processes providing compatibility across inconsistent networks stress the same aspects. In general, however, these sorts of standard are not common away from the IT realm. It might appear that the SSADM standard would fall into this category, specifying the process (method) of development; but as will be seen in Chapters 5 and 6, this would be mistaken.

Conceptual/product and conceptual/process standards, since they address future-oriented, widely defined requirements, are particularly appropriate to the IS domain. Indeed they are beginning to appear in more traditional arenas as technological innovation destabilizes conventional manufacturing processes and materials. There is a risk in developing such standards, since the basis may be too vague or remote for any widespread appeal or support. A fair indication of likely success might be the level of interest shown in the initial idea for such a standard. Thus the work on establishing agreed specifications for environments (e.g. portable common tools environment (PCTE)), data repositories (e.g. information resource dictionary standard (IRDS)) and data architectures (e.g. CASE data interchange format (CDIF)) generated initial interest and support from suppliers and users keen to ensure compatibility across diverse products. No single supplier felt capable of developing and enforcing their own solution.

In rare cases, with lack of widespread external support, a proprietary solution may be developed at high risk—but with potentially high returns if the demand grows once the solution is available. IBM's AD/Cycle is perhaps a salutary lesson in the inadvisability of such attempts in the complex and intangible aspects of the IS domain.

Essentially the conceptual standards mentioned by Cargill parallel Gabel's ideas of network integration. They arise increasingly in a fragmented, non-monopoly market where different networks must be integrated, but where it is extremely improbable that any single supplier can exert dominance. Thus network competition is unlikely to result in the emergence of a *de facto* standard, and the only feasible solution is for all the main network providers to coordinate the emergence of a neutral network, with minimal migration costs. Projects such as CDIF, IRDS, PCTE, and the like appear to offer low-cost/high-benefit solutions, since they are designed in part to act as gateways rather than as distinct networks themselves. (At the time of writing [mid-1994] only PCTE seems to be progressing towards a standard. Both of the other two initiatives have stalled, or been abandoned by key interest groups, and consequently lost direction and momentum. In Gabel's terms there is simply too much on the cost side of developing these highly complex and possibly short-lived gateways or frameworks—with far too little obvious benefit.)

Cargill's model provides a useful basis for considering different types of standard, and various strategies for achieving standardization. But he recognizes that the most predominant factor will be the importance placed on standards development by those involved in the process itself.

Motivations will vary, as will the depths of belief and conviction of individual participants. It will even happen that participation is premised on a defensive attitude, intending that either parts or the whole of the standard should founder, in order that it be severely weakened or limited in effect.

The success of the process of standards development will depend increasingly on shared convictions about the standard as such, and about the role of standards in general. Cargill argues that this realization has grown and matured in the IT arena, encompassing both suppliers and customers, and that this has been achieved by an increasing representation from technically proficient contributors. This has enhanced the tendency to arrive at pragmatic standards, as opposed to aiming at delivering paragons. 'Perfect standards are no longer the goal; instead, the focus is on obtaining a workable and acceptable standard within a time frame that will allow it to be useful' (Cargill, 1989, p. 41). This may be true for selected sections of IT, but it must also be observed that this has not yet come about in the wider realm of IS.

Like Gabel, Cargill is at pains to stress the role of the market in producing pressures for standards. Where Gabel offers a framework for understanding standards, Cargill focuses on the context within which they can be developed and applied. He embellishes his definition of a standard accordingly:

> A standard, of any form or type, represents a statement by its authors, who believe that their work will be understood, accepted and implemented by the market. This belief is tempered by the understanding that the market will act in its own best interests, even if these do not coincide with the standard. A standard is also one of the agents used by the standardization process to bring about market change.   (Cargill, 1989, pp. 41–2)

This supports and extends Gabel's concept of standards as providing mechanisms for different products and services to combine.

GABEL AND CARGILL—A SUMMARY

The work of Gabel and Cargill, taken as a whole, provides a focus on areas of IT product standardization, with Gabel providing material from areas other than IT, and Cargill discussing more than IT products. This offers a basis for some observations about the IS area more generally.

Gabel's work is particularly valuable in explaining the different pressures that might result in the emergence of a standard as a route to compatibility. Cargill, on the other hand, is more concerned with defining the range of different types of standard, and guiding IT standards makers in their deliberations.

Gabel's focus on competitive aspects of the emergence of compatibility extends Cargill's distinction between voluntary and regulatory standards. Apart from standards concerned with safety and other features of protection, which are typically regulatory, most other standards are voluntary in the sense that the suppliers and customers can choose whether or not to invoke and enforce them. But this is to use the term 'voluntary' in rather a strange sense; and to ignore the point that in a market context of any kind there will always be compelling reasons to adopt one strategy over another with regard to standards in general and compatibility in particular. (The UK public sector, like many other public sectors in other countries, is in a slightly different position since certain standards are mandatory.)

Gabel tends to ignore standards concerned with safety and protection, but then his main interest is in compatibility rather than standards as such. Cargill aims to encompass all aspects of IT standardization. His regulatory category tends to be entirely what he terms implementation standards— both process and product. These will also often be associated with some form of measurement as an indication that the standard has been met.

The non-regulatory types will tend to be either implementation/product, conceptual/product or conceptual/process. The implementation/product type conforms to the concept of a standard as a consistent and predictable expectation: it may be either an open and proprietary standard (e.g. IBM PC), or a restricted and proprietary standard (e.g. Windows). These will tend to be standards that have emerged as a result of network competition.

The conceptual/product and conceptual/process types will be future oriented. The former type will often be the result of strategies from both suppliers and consumers aimed at the development of a neutral network, or a higher-level gateway across supplier-based products. The conceptual/ process type will tend to be consumer led, often initiated by public sector bodies or the like.

If the realm of IT is extended to IS (ISE/IM), then the implementation/ process type has some relevance, since to some extent SSADM and other methods are non-regulatory standards of this kind (but as will be seen in Chapters 5 and 6 this is not entirely true). The main forms of process standard in IS will tend to be those associated with quality and certification aspects of systems features of products, or with models of lifecycle processes and procedures; these will almost always be conceptual rather than implementation specific.

While Gabel and Cargill are correct to stress the market-based pressures on standards, such arguments cannot be used to account for all standards issues. The market is an imperfect and unbalanced mechanism. Equally it is important not to lose sight of the internal factors in an organization which will lead to the articulation of standards needs. To some extent this will develop with the growing *maturity*, both of the organization itself and the external market. The next chapter deals with both of these issues, and outlines the concept of maturity in IS/IT, describing the process maturity model which itself forms the basis for work on a group of conceptual/ process type standards called SPICE.

3

STANDARDS AND MATURITY

BEYOND THE MARKET-BASED ARGUMENT—MARKET IMBALANCES AND OTHER IMPERFECTIONS

Even allowing for all the caveats raised earlier regarding standards and standardization in the IS realm, it may still be asked why the priorities and requirements relating to IS should be linked to standards at all? Statements regarding openness and procurement strategies explain the general case clearly and adequately. But they perhaps assume a greater knowledge and understanding of the nature of standards than most of their target audience possess. In addition, as Cargill notes, most often standards do not take account of the different orientations of customer and supplier (1989, pp. 46–7). The 'intelligent customer' may not be as abundant as some would wish; likewise the 'responsible supplier'.

Offering an explanation of types of standards, including their range from the authoritative and formal (and mandatory) to the voluntary and *de facto*, does not clarify the role standards can play. It also fails to address the specific areas in which standards can deliver a net benefit (and to whom); and equally to stress where the absence of workable standards produces a net liability. This is a critical shortcoming given the key role of social or behavioural aspects in standards making. Standards makers have to take a key role in an educative endeavour to rectify this situation.

Likewise if the establishment of any form of consensus is to be meaningful, then the standardization process must allow for the imbalances between potentially critical contributors to standards development. Suppliers, aware that they cannot control the market directly, will often target standards as the next best route for increasing the influence of their products and services. Furthermore, they will wish to constrain like-minded competitors from establishing their products as standards. Standards makers here will have to play a balancing role.

Users and consumers, on the other hand, will tend to be far too dispersed and diffuse to be able to combine and pursue an identifiable range of interests, unless there is already a recognized and accepted user-based forum in existence. Even if this is the case, participation in standards making is time consuming and resource intensive.

This is where the concept of the market as a collection of equally resourced individuals breaks down. Gabel recognizes this to some extent in his discussion of network economies and market dominance, but both he and Cargill are too ready to allow ill-defined market pressures to correct market-derived imbalances.

This is not the place to contribute to the argument on balancing markets, freedoms, and responsibilities; but it is important to recognize the tension between seeing standards as one way of controlling the market, and at the same time to see standards as emanating from the market. This then adds a further layer of responsibility to standards makers to represent diverse and disjointed interest groups.

Ironically one of the reasons why such imbalances have not appeared as starkly in some segments of the IS/IT domain is that both suppliers and users have retained a high level of scepticism with respect to the efficacy and power of standards. Developments around the PC, and in the realm of communications grouped around the development of OSI, however, indicate that the power of standards may be achieving wider acknowledgment. As Gray argues:

> standards *will* come and they *will* ultimately dominate the marketplace. There is now too much momentum behind them, and too many users who want and need them.   (1991, p. 43, italics in original)

Taken as a whole, the IS realm is immature with regard to standards: there are many competing standards (formal and informal) in some areas, none in others. Many activities continue with no regard to standards at all. Furthermore there are significant imbalances in the willingness and ability of key interest groups to participate in standards activities. Rectifying these anomalies will involve both a more targeted and precise campaign of explanation and support, together with a higher level of visibility of benefit from the accomplishment of successful standards making. The prime impetus for this must come from those who already appreciate the important role that standards can play. Whether they are willing and capable of doing this is another matter.

Any such campaign would have to contend with the problem that most of the standards in the IS realm have tended to concentrate on the developer and supplier perspectives, rather than satisfying the requirements of users and consumers. Hence most IT standards have concentrated on specific products and to a lesser extent processes. This has been at the expense of user perspectives, that demand a service-oriented range of standards, or at least process ones that include use and purchase aspects (see Chapter 4).

This results in a situation where standards are relevant and understandable to technicians and practitioners, but cannot be readily related to user and business issues. It may be that some standards, or aspects of standards, do have to be couched in technical terms. But the situation is further exacerbated by the location of key IS issues within standards bodies whose remit is fundamentally technical.

At the international level IS issues are almost tacitly assumed within the Software Engineering subcommittee, a predominantly technical forum. Even the newly promulgated CEN ISE committee (TC311) reports to BTS7, a body primarily concerned with technical standards such as those for metering and card-readers.

Similarly frameworks that do attempt to deal with information systems development (ISD), as opposed to software development, still tend to be product and process biased. The Framework for Information Systems Development (Heym and Osterle, 1991) broadly classifies the ISD domain along three axes—application type, lifecycle perspective, method focus— with no focus for the service aspect of the system itself. Although such frameworks are a useful basis for further work, in general they all suffer from such limitations.

THE IS SERVICE VIEW

Essentially the service view of an IS is in need of articulation. Centred very much within the user-based perspective, one definition of an IS is a 'set of *organized procedures* that, when executed, *provide information* for *decision making*, *communications*, and/or *control* of the organization'. Service-based and consumer-oriented standards in the IS area must address these issues.

The ISD perspective, although ultimately linked to the service provision, has its own characteristics. One definition of ISD states that it is '*a change process* taken with respect to *object systems* in a set of *environments* by a *development group* to achieve or maintain some *objectives*' (Lyytinen, 1987, italics added). Each of the emphasized terms can be distinguished, and critical factors in accomplishing or dealing with each designated. This then begins to chart the main activities involved in ISD, and hints at the role of standards in facilitating each aspect of the entire process.

In general IS standards are required to enhance and support predictability, planning and control in the provision and support of an IS. Essentially IS management, and information management itself, can be characterized by a threefold view consisting of planning, organization, and control. Technical problems as such do not impinge unless they affect one or more of these aspects. The three relate to one another in a hierarchy of importance: planning being more important than organization, which is more important than control (see Fig. 3.1).

Figure 3.1 Hierarchy of planning, organization, and control.

A TYPOLOGY OF STANDARDS

Not all standards serve the same purpose, or are of the same type. A useful fourfold distinction gives the categories of *product, process, resource, notation*. Recognizing that standards can vary from authoritative statements of (mandatory) features (*must*) to recommendations of practice (*should*) and guidelines (*may*), the different types of standard can be described as follows:

- A product standard will define what comprises the complete and acceptable features of a specified product.
- A process standard will define the procedures or techniques necessary to develop a product or achieve an objective.
- A resource standard describes the attributes, utilization, and constraints of a resource.
- A notation standard describes the characteristics of formal interchanges between persons involved in IS development, provision, and use.

In general, for IS standards, product and notation standards will tend more towards the mandatory statement, whereas resource and process ones will tend to be recommendations and guidelines.

This means that there will be a larger role for interpretation and experience in implementing and enforcing process and resource standards, than there will be for the others. This is not to imply that one form of standard is more important than another. Although it has been true to say that the defining and enforcement of notation standards has been by far the most straightforward, since transgression is clearly testable, e.g. with compilers. Although one can produce typologies of standards, ultimately the application and recognition of such standards will be dependent upon the sorts of market pressures discussed by Cargill, Gabel, and Gray, but it will also be dependent upon other factors, particularly those concerned with the characteristics of organizations themselves. These characteristics are best conceived of in terms of the *maturity* of the organization itself.

IS MATURITY

It was stated earlier that the IS arena as a whole is immature with regard to standards. In order to substantiate this, it is necessary to take a wider view and explain how developments in IS issues and activities can be conceived as charting a process of growth and maturation.

Everyone would agree that the development of computer and communications technology since the 1960s has been astounding. The power and availability of the machinery has led to its permeation of increasingly larger aspects of social and organizational activities: from an initially limited and specialized base has arisen a focus and characterizing theme of the last quarter of the 20th century. Although it is far more contentious to say that we live in the information age, it is not inherently absurd to recognize that the twin technologies of computing and communication influence and modify many aspects of our collective existence. But how best can this development be understood, particularly if we are to draw conclusions for the future?

The use of the term 'development' is deliberately neutral, merely implying some form of change over a period of time, rather than the more value-laden 'progress' or 'advance'. More common in the burgeoning literature in this field is to find the use of terms such as 'growth', 'maturation', and 'evolution'. These have explicitly quantitative and qualitative aspects: the technology has flourished, both in terms of its extent and the characteristics of its implementation and application. There are more people making use of the technology, in a wider variety of ways, and with greater effect. (In the context of my present argument I shall ignore for the moment those who would dispute the essentially beneficial nature of such developments—but see Bryant, 1991.)

What the proponents of such optimistic views need to offer is some theoretical background to support their opinion of the nature and trajectory of the advance of the technology. What characterized the initial phase of the 1960s? What has changed since then? Where is the change likely to end? Are the changes mostly quantitative or qualitative? Is the trajectory one of degree or is the essential nature of the technology altered?

Certainly by the late 1960s it was apparent that the benefits brought by computer technology did not come without cost, and a variety of international conferences and publications proclaimed the existence of a software crisis—a call echoing to the present time. To the technical specialists, and software systems project managers, this crisis manifested itself in the widening gap between hardware and software in terms of reliability and price/performance ratios. To the organizational executive the problem was balancing and justifying the increased demand for resources to complete computer systems projects with the expectations and desires of the user community. These twin crises had a common cause: the unplanned, overambitious, and rapid expansion in the use of a previously highly specialized and constrained technology.

GIBSON AND NOLAN'S 'S-CURVE'

In 1973–4 Gibson and Nolan offered an explanatory and predictive model of the stages involved in the adoption of computer use in organizations (many of these papers are reprinted in Nolan, 1982). The model was based on research of several large US corporations, and treated their dollar expenditure on computer technology as an indicator of technological development, or what would now be termed IT development. The trend for expenditure showed that it followed a familiar S-shaped curve (Fig. 3.2): an organizational learning curve.

Gibson and Nolan argued that the curve could be seen as composed of four stages, although later models expanded this to six. A brief discussion of the model, and its aftermath, is relevant to the present discussion, since it outlines some of the key features in the development of the technology for IS, stressing not simply the advance of the technological wizardry, but the necessity for organizations to evolve to accommodate to and adapt the technology itself.

The six-stage model, with its incorporation of the concept of 'maturity', provides a basis for appreciating that organizations have to grow, *learn*, and develop with a changing environment and culture. The model, as extended by later critics, also emphasizes certain organizational and contextual

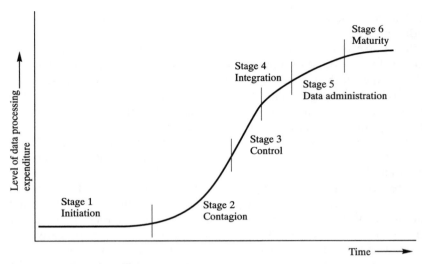

Figure 3.2 Gibson and Nolan's six-stage model.

characteristics that are crucial for standards issues, and which link the early Nolan model to the later maturity model of Humphrey and his associates.

The first stage of the Nolan model was shown by the gently rising part of the S-curve, indicating the period of *initiation*, following computer acquisition. Here people were gradually gaining familiarity with the technology as it was introduced into their organizational environment. This is a stage of experiment and pilot project, with little planning or control—'the computer will shock the organization' (Nolan, 1982, p. 14). In many instances, the first systems to be targeted will be those that are already partially automated or integrated with well-established rules and procedures, but where there is a large volume of repetitive work, i.e. aspects of bookkeeping, account reporting, and so on.

Once others in the organization see the value and power of the technology, they start to make demands for its implementation in their work. In addition, there may be high-level decisions to permit or encourage a degree of investigation and experimentation with the new technology. This leads to the second stage of *contagion*, or 'intense systems development', where the number and range of applications dramatically rises. There is little or no attempt to manage this growth, and the costs of the developments and associated efforts are borne as organizational overheads rather than as charges. This stimulates demand and leads to increased spending. The rate of increase is significantly higher than for the earlier stage, and inevitably results in a budgetary crisis and calls to account for the expenditure.

This is the start of the third stage, *control*: 'Management mobilizes a set of tasks to control expenditures for computing' (Nolan, 1982, p. 16). This usually means that budgetary controls are introduced for any purchase of new equipment. There is also established a prioritization of application development projects and requests for new applications. There is an accompanying imposition of project control and planning for the application development area as a whole. All of these practices put a brake on expenditure, leading to a levelling-off or sometimes even a slight fall in the total. This is also often reinforced by the introduction of charging procedures for applications work. 'In the extreme case, the computer organization may be assigned profit centre responsibility' (p. 17).

Nolan makes the point that the 'myriad of control devices' associated with this stage is 'often an overreaction with strong forces toward centralization' (p. 17). On the other hand, it is precisely this forceful response to the budgetary crisis that can be a basis for promoting enforcement of (informal) standards, documentation and reporting practices, and the like.

The fourth stage, *integration*, represents an emergence from the tight regulation of the preceding stage. There is a general realization of what is involved in 'managing the data resource'. The role of the computer system in assisting the organization achieve its objectives becomes more appreciated. This necessitates a move away from seeing the technology in purely technical or mechanistic terms, and a growing realization that the organizational and user perspectives must be taken into consideration. Part of this maturation will be evident in the gradual erosion of distinctions between user domains and their related computer-based applications.

This four-stage model was later expanded into six stages, with the addition of *data administration* and *technological maturity* as extensions of the integration stage. Partly this was a result of the advances in technology in the late 1970s, particularly database technology, which promised to resolve the conflict between a centralized data resource, and specific and unique applications utilizing and amending some of that data.

The existence of, or potential for, a true database extended the stage of integration into that of data administration. Data, rather than applications development, becomes the key, and the ideas of resource management drive the organizational perspective, with concomitant effects on budgeting, control, planning, and so on. One of the key features of this stage is that responsibility for the overall data processing type function is extended to users, who begin to form alliances across traditional departmental divides. Non-specialist participation in development and aspects of end-user responsibility are often introduced at this point.

All these features, if fully evolved and coordinated, lead to the nirvana of technological maturity. At this point there is overall recognition of the role of the data resource in the organization—users and specialists alike accepting joint responsibility and accountability in development and

Table 3.1 Nolan's six-stage model

Stage	Control		Objective of control
	Computer	Data	
1	Low		no control
2	Low		facilitate growth
3	High		contain supply
4		Low	match supply and demand
5		High	contain demand
6		High	balance supply and demand

operation of the applications portfolio. The strategy for the data resource is adapted to the overall organizational strategy.

Nolan characterized the six stages as shown in Table 3.1. The Gibson–Nolan model was widely accepted for a number of years, although its status was never clarified by the authors themselves. Was it historically specific, applying only to the period under review—the 1960s and 1970s—or did it hold for other periods? In other words, would an organization starting to adopt IT in the late 1970s or early 1980s have to mirror the six stages, or could they plan for quicker and easier routes to stages 4 and 5? Could parts of an organization learn more quickly than other parts?

Other criticisms levelled at the model questioned the approach and method of the basic research, in particular whether budgets were a reliable and consistent indicator of IT development. 'A change in budgets is unlikely to act as a surrogate to such a wide range of variables, and that, further, DP budgets tend to increase in a linear manner and are not S-shaped over time' (see Jackson, 1986, p. 52, where he lists some key criticisms).

In his discussion of the Nolan model, Jackson concluded that, despite the criticisms and weaknesses of the model, 'It represents a bold attempt to explain the complexities of technological change' (p. 52). This seems a sound assessment, and certainly the Nolan model has been instrumental in directing people's attention to the sorts of organizational issues previously neglected or not associated with IT developments. But by the mid-1980s, with the spread of the PC, any simple application of the Nolan model was impossible. Jackson, however, argued that the model still applies if the vertical axis is changed to reflect 'the degree of technology penetration' in an organization: 'or, more simply, "technological maturity"' (p. 53).

TECHNOLOGICAL MATURITY AND TECHNOLOGICAL DIFFUSION

Technological maturity aligns Nolan's model with the later work of, for instance, McFarlan and McKenney. Their work was derived from analyses of 28 organizations, and sought to characterize the domain as one of 'managing technological diffusion' (Jackson, 1986, p. 53). This produced a model of four types of technological use, or orientation: technological identification and innovation; technological learning and adaptation; rationalization and management control; maturity and widespread technology transfer (Jackson maps these onto the Nolan S-curve as shown in Fig. 3.3).

The key to McFarlan and McKenney's approach is that it can be applied to individual technologies, even if they are closely related to other technologies, and it is quite likely that all four aspects can be observed in any organization at any one time. This is partly to argue that technological diffusion is a complex process, with each new technology setting new problems at the same time as it offers solutions to old problems. It is also perhaps to indicate that organizations fail to generalize and apply their learning, going through similar stages with microcomputers, for instance, as they had earlier done with mainframes. Organizations learn (from) their mistakes; and repeat them in new contexts.

The overall significance of Nolan's and McFarlan and McKenney's work (among others) is that the introduction and use of technology has to be planned and managed. On the other hand, such work also points to the necessary *unplanned-ness* of the early stages of technological diffusion, where too strict a regime may well stifle the innovative potential of such

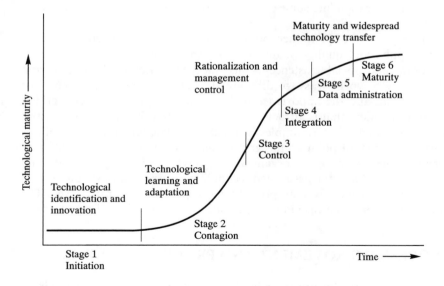

Figure 3.3 Mapping technological maturity on to Gibson and Nolan's model (based on Jackson, 1986).

developments. Innovation must be encouraged at the same time as its ramifications may have to be contained or carefully cultivated.

An early phase of experimentation must be followed by some form of consolidation, generalizing from both positive and negative experiences in order to plan and organize for the future, i.e. to start to develop standards. This is to argue that standards should not play this sort of constraining role early in the development of a technology, but must develop once the rate of innovation has begun to fall, or needs to be controlled.

For example, in the case of the present state of object-oriented approaches, although there is a bewildering array of notations, terminologies, and types and applications of object orientation, it is often argued that it is too soon to seek an object-oriented orthodoxy or consensus. The concepts and their applicability are simply too unstable and untried. Any attempt to impose a wide-reaching standard would be bound to fail, or might stifle genuine advances in the technology.

On the other hand, in the realm of IS development methods, a level of stability has been reached, and there are grounds for arguing that certain standards for notations, techniques, and methods themselves are appropriate.

The Nolan model lays the basis for a consideration of the role of standards once IS/IT development has gained some momentum in an organization. Although the original model was primarily focused on IT in the sense of the hardware and components, the later work of McFarlan and McKenney in expanding some of these ideas points to its applicability to the wider context of IS.

This expansion of IT to incorporate IS resulted in the realization that the flow, supply, and quality of information was critical to many aspects of corporate and social existence. Thus another aspect of McFarlan and McKenney's work was to distinguish between the main types of organization, and the importance of IS/IT to each. Their strategic grid is one of those ideas that is attractive at first sight, but then leads to a host of reservations and counterexamples (see Jackson, 1986, for a discussion of this work). The overall point of the grid is that it demonstrates that different organizations, or parts of organizations, have diverse requirements and priorities for IS and the associated technology. Furthermore simply buying in the latest technology may provoke more problems than it solves. The same may also be the case in the application or invocation of standards.

PROCESS IMPROVEMENT AND PROCESS MATURITY

There are considerable pressures in all types of organization to maintain or develop expertise and excellence in all aspects of corporate and social life. The quality culture has been imported from Japan and elsewhere and applied to a wide variety of (un)suitable aspects. One of the general features of this development was that things had to be defined and measurable in order that they could be assessed and then improved. This tended to assume the existence of convention and procedural predictability—a *process architecture*. Without this there was no way of ascertaining when things were going wrong, being over-resourced, or failing in some way.

Much of the work on quality has concentrated on *process improvement*. This is based on the idea that rather than checking or certifying that the final product meets some set of criteria, it is preferable to ensure that the production process itself is effective, efficient, well managed, and monitored. Thus the full range of types of standard mentioned previously are relevant since product, process, resource, and notation must all be assessed against some pertinent form of 'desired objective'.

Some standards need to be invoked to measure the effectiveness of the process, others will be used to indicate what aspects of specific products need to be measured or assessed. The results of product assessment will be fed back into the production process, with the identification and eradication of the key sources of errors and poor quality as the objective.

These ideas of statistical process control and process improvement contributed to the total quality philosophy of zero defects and continuous improvement. Unfortunately, although this aim is superficially attractive and laudable, it fails to take account of many aspects of organizational reality, particularly in the realm of IS.

More critically, many of the prescribed routes to total quality fail to account for the position from which organizations begin their improvement programmes. Crosby (1979), addressing the general topic of quality, suggested that organizations cannot simply embark upon wholesale process improvement strategies, hoping to reach new heights of excellence in quantum bounds. There must be the realization that there is a range of improvement that must be effected in some realistic sequence: 'learning to walk before trying to run'. Humphrey (1989) adapted Crosby's and Deming's (1982) ideas and applied them to the development of software with his model of process maturity.

The Software Process Maturity Model (SPMM) was derived from the work of Crosby and indirectly from the ideas of Deming—in particular the notions of process improvement and statistically based control of the main production activities. These are now seen as some of the base concepts underlying the total quality (TQ) movement, with its stress on continuing improvement against measured standards of achievement.

The SPMM, now also in the slightly amended form of the Capability Maturity Model (CMM), represents the most sustained attempt to extend the TQ perspective to software-based systems. This is not a simple task, since the production-based assumptions of TQ do not transfer easily to the processes of information systems and software development.

Following Crosby closely, the key idea of the SPMM (CMM) approach is that the *process* of software production is the key feature requiring attention and improvement. As such, SPMM is concerned primarily with one of the three main ideas behind the development of software engineering: the management aspect (the other two being productivity and reliability). This is not to say that the SPMM focus precludes the other two, but it does place them lower in the sequence of priorities for improvement activities.

More critically, it makes these other facets dependent on the primary one: increased productivity and higher reliability will only follow from better management of the development process itself. There may be other avenues for developing more reliable software and doing so more efficiently, but these improvements will be at best transitory unless the process infrastructure develops along the lines of the maturity model.

This has implications for any innovation or improvement strategy in software engineering in general, and by extension to the entire domain of ISE. Since the SPMM approach is firmly based on improving management as a necessary first step leading to improvements in other aspects, it lays critical stress on the establishment of guidelines and procedures. Furthermore, any changes or innovations in procedures, tools, or technology become potential obstacles or at best hindrances in process improvement. This is hardly surprising since any innovation ought to be recognized as a critical occurrence in organizational routine and activities, though this is often forgotten in the rush to innovate and acquire the latest technology—particularly with regard to IT.

The application of IT itself has ramifications far beyond the technology, and its successful utilization is dependent upon a whole host of features and prerequisites. The same principles apply to the introduction of technology as they do to the process of software development itself. The perspective of SPMM/CMM illustrates these issues specifically for software development.

The concept of maturity in the SPMM parallels that from the Nolan and McFarlan and McKenney models. In SPMM, however, the five-stage model is one of strict and almost inescapable sequence: organizational practices and procedures must develop through the five stages in order. As the literature on SPMM, CMM and SPICE (Software Process Improvement and Capability dEtermination–an ISO project concerned with the delivery of a set of standards based on SPMM) is plentiful, what follows is only a brief outline of the general principles of SPMM relevant to the present discussion.

In his original work, Humphrey's main objective was twofold:

- To provide guidance to consumers and procurement agencies in the selection of capable software contractors.
- To provide guidance to developers in their assessment of their own strengths and weaknesses with a view to process improvement.

The entire software task has to be treated 'as a process that can be controlled, measured and improved' (Humphrey, 1989, p. 4). This can be accomplished through six steps (p. 4):

1. Understand the current status of the development process(es).
2. Develop a vision of the desired process.
3. Establish a list of required process improvement actions in priority order.
4. Produce a plan to accomplish the required actions.
5. Commit resources to execute the plan.
6. Start again at step 1.

Humphrey's five-stage model is as follows (lowest first):

1. *Initial* There is little or no acknowledgement of routine procedures; everything is *ad hoc*. Statistical control is quite impossible since there is not even any rudimentary form of planning and monitoring. 'Change control is lax, and there is little senior management exposure or understanding of the problems and issues' (p. 6). This echoes many of the characteristics of Nolan's initiation and contagion stages—novelty, experimentation, lack of control, lack of planning, and lack of visibility to management.
2. *Repeatable* 'The organization has achieved a stable process with a repeatable level of statistical control by initiating rigorous project management of commitments, costs, schedules and changes' (p. 5). This parallels Nolan's control stage, as well as parts of the integration stage. The main achievement in reaching stage 2 is the ability to estimate and plan on the basis of previous experience. The problems arise when the present and future diverges from the past. 'Organizations at the Repeatable Process Level thus face major risks when they are presented with new challenges' (p. 8).
3. *Defined* Unlike the prior level, here there will be an understanding of the development process, allowing adaptation to and accommodation of novel projects and development contexts. Organizations at this level will be more capable of dealing with the unexpected.
4. *Managed* 'The organization has initiated comprehensive process measurements and analysis' (p. 5). This data gathering imposes considerable costs, but if processed carefully and honestly can indicate key areas for improvement and investment.
5. *Optimizing* 'The organization now has a foundation for continuing improvement and optimization of the process' (p. 5). Levels 3–5 correspond in part with Nolan's integration and data administration stages, Although Humphrey's level 5 is perhaps as remote as Nolan's technological maturity.

SPMM/CMM stresses the necessity to get the basic management structure perfected and in place before anything else. Project management, configuration management, and change control are essential prerequisites for any substantive and enduring advances. Only once these general management practices are in place can significant benefits result from application of technically specific methods and established procedures.

These rules and guidelines are components of a context-specific *process architecture*, which itself can form the basis for a defined and understood development process, robust enough to withstand widespread application and amendment. Later, and suitably embellished, it can provide a platform for the collection of project data for comparison and assessment of performance—and hence targets for improvement.

The inference from this is that much of the effort required for introducing information systems development methods, CASE technology, and various forms of standards will be dissipated if some form of process architecture is not in place and widely familiar to and accepted by development personnel. Moreover, the introduction of any change to such a guiding perspective will inevitably result in a slight deterioration of performance, if only in the short term.

Innovations in the form of methods and CASE tools must be viewed in this light. Some weight is lent to this argument by consideration of the adoption of even simple tools such as compilers, which was only feasible after programming practices and language syntax were established to some degree, often as a result of a standard syntax and set of programming practices being widely applied.

STANDARDS FOR DIFFERENT MATURITY LEVELS

Similarly the imposition of standards on a development environment must be planned accordingly. When an organization decides to apply, develop, or promote standards of any kind, it must ensure that the ones it imposes are appropriate and realistic to its own level of maturity.

There is little point having a standard in the sense of a *desired objective*, if the path from the present situation to the future objective is clouded in the mists of impractical and unrealistic aspirations. Improvement will only be effected if it is incremental and pragmatic—and seen to be so. At the initial level the most relevant standards will be those promoting established management practices, derived from other fields. Until recently this involved a somewhat haphazard translation of 'best practice' from non-IS/SE activities. Increasingly this deficiency has been remedied with the appearance of standards specifically directed at software development: software project management, software configuration management, and so on. Even so, at the very basic level there is a good deal of truth in

Humphrey's assertion that although software development is 'a new and unique field, traditional management methods can and should be used' (1989, p. 25).

In general at the lowest two stages of maturity the only standards to be considered should be those that Cargill defines as constraining and reinforcing (good) practices and (realistic) expectations; i.e. implementation standards, for both products and processes. These will have to be adopted with a view to changing the development environment, and aiming for the third level with a defined process. Only once this third level is in sight will it be worthwhile to consider developing or invoking conceptual standards. Humphrey is very clear that standards can only play a significant role once the repeatable level has been firmly established. The progress from level 1 to level 2 should result in an environment 'sufficiently stabilized to permit orderly process improvement' (p. 155). In order to effect the transition to level 3, 'the subjects requiring priority management attention at this point are standards, software inspections, testing, advanced configuration management topics, process models and architecture, and the Software Engineering Process Group' (p. 155).

Humphrey's use of the term standards is fairly specific, and firmly anchored in the software development context. (As will be seen in Chapter 4, this restriction to the product and process aspects of software development, while understandable, can and must be extended to other levels such as ISM in general, and also to service aspects of the system itself.) He introduces Deming's definition of standards and procedures as 'operational definitions: something everyone can communicate about and work toward' (p. 157). Humphrey then distinguishes between *guidelines, procedures, standards, conventions,* and *practices* (pp. 158–90), but generally these are in line with the definitions offered in Chapters 1 and 2.

The main reason Humphrey offers a range of terms is that he restricts the definition of a standard to a 'rule or basis for comparison that is used to assess size, content, or value, typically established by common practice or by a designated standards body' (p. 158). This is to confine the concept to the idea of a qualitative comparison, not surprising given his predisposition towards statistical process control. His other terms cover the other meanings of standard discussed earlier.

In fact, in the subsequent sections of his discussion, Humphrey extends the meaning of the term standard.

> Standards are needed when many people, products, or tools must coexist. They are essential for establishing common support environments, performing integration, or conducting systems test. Aron points out that 'large software organizations are finding that the value of one set of uniform procedures for the whole shop justifies a significant investment in training and procedure development'.   (p. 160)

In line with Humphrey's earlier point about software being unique, but still benefiting from traditional management methods, the converse also applies: Aron's justification for standards applies to organizations other than those involved in the development of software.

Unfortunately even Humphrey has to admit that there is little quantitative evidence to support the benefit of standards. On the other hand, he refers to several surveys of project managers which found that they invariably ranked standards as the most important source of solutions for the critical problems they regularly experienced—although there is no further evidence to show if specific standards did eventually deliver the promised solutions.

The introduction of standards must itself be regarded as a skill to be acquired and perfected at an individual level as well as at the project and organizational levels. The concept of maturity still applies, since the objective is a combination of experience and knowledge tempered by a sensitivity to the particular context, which in turn implies competence.

FROM ORGANIZATIONAL MATURITY TO INDIVIDUAL MATURITY AND COMPETENCE

A model based on the work of Hubert Dreyfus and Stuart Dreyfus provides at the individual level a complement to the organizational model of maturity. They seek to present an account of the route from *novice* to *expert* in the acquisition of general and specific skills. The development involves moving from initially learning and obeying strict rules, to an appreciation of contextual pressures, the role of intuition and reinterpretation of experience, and the inevitable ambiguity arising from the application of strict systems of rules in a wide variety of circumstances.

The model offers a hierarchy building from stage 1 (*novice*) to stage 5 (*expertise*). As a novice, starting the acquisition of a new skill, concentration is focused on objective facts and rigid rule-structures which can be recognized and appreciated without reference to external, contextual features. 'The novice nurse is taught how to read blood pressure, measure bodily outputs, and compute fluid retention, and is given rules for determining what to do when those measurements reach certain values' (Dreyfus and Dreyfus, 1986, p. 22). A basic syntax is imparted to the learner, but it is seen largely as an admixture of independent rules.

In stage 2 (*advanced beginner*), some experience of real situations has been acquired, and thus there is a basis for appreciation not only of strict rules, but of repeated patterns of events and features that may in part be context dependent. Using the example of the nurse, there will be the ability to distinguish different sounds and patterns of breathing, and to appreciate the possible causes behind them. But there will not yet be the ability to explain to others exactly how they differ, or perhaps even why they differ. This shifts from formal expressions of independent rules to the realization that adhering strictly to a single rule may impact upon other rules, and that 'rules of thumb' need to be developed. These latter rules are required both in the sense that rules about combinations of rules are needed, and that straightforward, indifferent application of rules may not be possible or sensible.

The next stage, *competence*, involves the skill to adopt a 'hierarchical procedure of decision making' (p. 24), predicated on a wider view of the situation, and a plan based on this appreciation. Again the example of the nurse illustrates the point. The competent nurse will not simply move through procedures and patients in a prescribed order, but will be able to assess priorities of need and sequences of treatment. Dreyfus and Dreyfus term this the 'combination of nonobjectivity and necessity'.

This implies the beginnings of a movement away from rule-based models of cognition to a contextually sensitive model. It is non-objective in the sense that the competent student starts to appreciate that any rule or body of rules cannot be applied mechanistically and heedlessly. Situations will occur in which rules will have to be broken or amended, or new ones invented.

Furthermore, the competent and intelligent actor does not wait until the sequence of events demands selection and application of a rule, or procedure, but plans ahead and makes decisions based on predictions and priorities. This introduces the aspect of self-awareness or reflexivity. The actor assesses, decides, and acts, taking responsibility for decisions and actions. It is not simply the case of disinterestedly and slavishly following rules laid down by others. This results in a shift away from the lower levels, where any error can be blamed on the rules themselves (or their inadequate scope or specification), to the position where the competent actor can regard decisions as involving aspects of personal responsibility. It is precisely this aspect that is often ignored in currently fashionable 'decisionistic' models of intelligence, for the most part derived from the work of Simon and his colleagues (1983), where intelligence is characterized as 'problem-solving' and restricted to impersonal (hence automatable) rule-like procedures.

For Dreyfus and Dreyfus there is certainly more to intelligence than mechanistic rule following. Their critique of artificial intelligence is founded precisely on developing an appreciation of the paucity of such constrained representations. The competent practitioner already transcends any decisionistic constraints; the next two levels take this further. Both are characterized by 'a rapid, fluid, involved kind of behaviour that bears no apparent similarity to the slow, detached reasoning of the problem-solving process' (p. 27).

The major distinguishing feature of stages 4 and 5 (*proficiency* and *expertise*) is the ability to assess situations holistically, intuitively. The proficient performer will still operate analytically, but within an intuitive understanding and organizing of the situation. The expert will not even need this partial level of analytical activity if the situation is within the realms of normality and familiarity. The expert can function without recourse to conscious, analytic reasoning; the skills are intuitive, instinctive, automatic. Dreyfus and Dreyfus give a dramatic illustration of this with regard to an expert chess player being given the task of adding numbers spoken to him at a rate of one number per second, while playing five-seconds-a-move chess against a player of only slightly lesser ability, and convincingly beating his opponent.

The Dreyfus and Dreyfus model might seem to undermine the efficacy and importance of standards. After all, the expert will have no need of standards as such, since experts can operate intuitively and holistically. It might be argued that only at the lower skill levels will standards be required, initially as part of a prescriptive framework for beginners, and later as the basis on which relatively proficient but inexperienced developers can make decisions.

This is to fall into the trap of seeing standards as easy solutions to difficult problems. Given the complexity of the ISE domain, and the vast array of standards (*de facto*, *de jure*, and *potential*) which are or might be applicable, it is crucial that professional developers exhibit precisely the higher levels of competence demanded by the Dreyfus and Dreyfus model.

In fact many of the problems and bad experiences of (particularly *de facto*) standards use arise because standards users fail to get beyond the lowest level of skill: interpreting standards as prescriptive injunctions to be adhered to completely and precisely, with little reference to context and other factors.

In laying the blame for bad standards and bad standards practices at the door of the standards makers, Cargill may well have had exactly these sorts of failings in mind. Many of the IS/IT standards initiatives are now having to address the problems of guidance in the use of standards rather than simply the technical aspects of the standards documents themselves. The Dreyfus and Dreyfus model seems to offer a basis to explain and remedy people's difficulties in standards application and combination.

APPLYING THE LESSONS OF MATURITY

The SPMM/CMM model does offer a model for the development and adoption of standards. But does it apply only to software developers? It certainly applies to more than software, since the whole concept of a defined process must encompass the context within which the software development is taking place. If the organization is a software supplier, the application of the SPMM is fairly straightforward. If, on the other hand, the model is applied to an in-house organization, the range of activities must encompass the alignment between the full IS function (whatever departmental title it has) and the rest of the organization. This will also hold for those organizations that have out-sourced key components of their IS function.

The model also has application to those involved in procuring systems, and not merely in the sense that they will wish to assess the capability of potential suppliers. Using the ideas from the various maturity models and the Dreyfus and Dreyfus skill model, the procurement process must account for competences within the customer/purchaser organization. The organization must understand how the software to be supplied is to be used in and conform to the activities in the host environment. Also there must be some expertise in using and applying any relevant standards. There is little point in assessing the capability of suppliers if the in-house IS staff and users are incapable of incorporating the delivered system into their organizational routine. (*Procured by the professional; designed and built by the expert; operated by the incompetent.*)

The process maturity approach illustrates the necessity for effecting the progression from creating the basic management infrastructure to developing or articulating a process architecture. This will apply to the wider IS context just as much as it clearly does to the software development context.

Humphrey limits most of his discussion to very specific software standards, mostly product or process based, and his examples are drawn from internal standards programmes. The next chapter will argue that the product and process perspective has to be extended to incorporate service aspects of IS. But the model also needs to be augmented to apply to a fuller range of standards, and to the IS realm in general.

Given the extended domain of IS, the main changes to the maturity model need to take account of the context within which the software development is taking place. Thus the introduction of general management features such as change control, project management, and so on will have to derive from those practices in other parts of the organization. The derivation of a model of normal procedures will likewise have to link to the host organization, and the ways in which it accepts delivery of IS products and uses IS services. The final three stages of the Nolan model are a guide to the sorts of characteristics that need to be cultivated.

Rather than simply trying to invent a process architecture, and link in the standards once it is established, it may be quicker and simpler to adopt external practices and enforce public standards. Process standards may often be seen as embodiments of 'best practice', although care must be taken that the practice is relevant to the target environment. Some standards may also offer a basis for comparative assessment. Attempts to promote process improvement in this way may engender problems of innovation.

If such problems can be resolved, or better still avoided altogether, then developers will themselves be able to progress on an individual level, and the whole organization can start to achieve maturity and new levels of confidence. This will be demonstrated by more profound and flexible use of specific practices, while still remaining compliant to standards.

This overall strategy for improvement is based on another key feature of standards: that they must be useful—pragmatic devices rather than quixotic paragons. Standards have a dual role to play in the IS context, and the maturity models emphasize them both. First they must embody excellence: 'Do it this way because otherwise you will make the same mistakes as your predecessors and precursors.' Secondly, the ability to use and apply standards in combination with, and an understanding of the specific context demonstrates reaching a certain stage of maturity.

In these first three chapters I have sought to outline a variety of views on standards, and then to locate them within a maturity framework. Now it is time to move to a more extended discussion on IS and quality; and then on to the details of the SSADM standard itself.

4

STANDARDS FOR SERVICE AND QUALITY IN INFORMATION SYSTEMS ENGINEERING

In the previous chapters an information system was defined as a system whose objective and functions encompass the gathering, accepting, processing, storing, retrieving, producing, and presenting of information. It was further stated that any such provision must be relevant to an organization, in such a way that the information is accessible and useful to those who wish to use it, including managers, staff, clients, and other interested stakeholders. The functions of the IS may be enacted by differing combinations of people and devices—the latter increasingly and predominantly based around information and communications technology (IT). Above all, the information that is the object of these activities must be of relevance within the (organizational) context within which the IS operates.

Although the subsequent chapters will concentrate specifically on a standard for an IS development *method*, this should not obscure the importance of the service aspect—the persistent and continuous characteristic of an IS. If the service afforded by an information system fails or falls below users' thresholds of acceptance, then it will not matter very much how well it was developed in the first place.

Parts of this chapter are derived from sections of Bryant and Grogan (1993).

Developing standards for services, as opposed to products or processes, is still in its very early stages, both within the IS domain and everywhere else. Some work has been done within the BSI/DISC IST branch, specifically within the Software Engineering committee (IST/15). The work is designed to provide a framework for standardization activities aimed at service aspects in general, not limited merely to IS/IT service aspects in particular. Inevitably any discussion of standards and service tends to move quickly to focus on 'quality', and it is to this that we now turn.

QUALITY AND INFORMATION SYSTEMS

The application of models of quality to the IS realm is fraught with difficulty—which is not to imply that it is uncomplicated in other areas. The transformation of concepts such as quality control, quality assurance, and quality inspection cannot be readily applied to many of the key features of IS. This is a result of an IS embodying aspects of planning, management, and control, as well as being a focus and resource for social and organizational interaction. Moreover the system must provide a service to the extent that it satisfies demands of its users, or a significant subset thereof.

The service, however, can only be provided once the system, or a significant component, is in place. This is no trivial matter, and hence the development process itself must be a topic for quality assessment. Furthermore, the range of skills and intervening users of information systems development (ISD) deliverables is considerable, and the full variety of distinct *quality horizons* must be incorporated.

Finally, assuming that a key component of the eventual IS is automated— hardware, software, communications—there is a more tangible product-based view of quality relevant to the discussion. Each of these aspects has distinct ramifications.

The application of quality issues and assessment to the area of IS must take account of this complex nature of IS development and continuity. Any discussion of IS standards must encompass this complexity—IS development process, IS products, IS service.

THE IS DEVELOPMENT PROCESS

The IS development process cannot merely be considered as a technical issue, devoid of social ramifications. Welke offers a definition of IS development as a 'change process taken with respect to object systems in a set of environments by a development group to achieve or maintain some objectives' (quoted in Lyytinen, 1987, p. 6). Lyytinen amplifies this in his discussion of systems development issues, offering a tripartite hierarchy of different 'object systems contexts'—respectively technology, language, organization. The technology context is seen as the underlying one, on which rests the language context, with the organization context at the top.

This model offers a useful orientation for a discussion of the key issues of applying standards and quality programmes to IS. The linguistic and organizational facets reinforce the position that quality is not simply a technical feature, a case of fine tuning and unconscious application of rules. It also undermines the belief that slavish adherence to a prescriptive set of standards embodying detailed procedures and associated techniques will produce a quality system. Those with any experience of actual systems development will know that this is an untenable expectation.

In any case IS methodologies do not offer this sort of intricate guidance and constraining, detailed instruction. Again Lyytinen provides a definition of a methodology which affords a more amenable basis for further consideration:

> An information systems development methodology (ISDM) is an organized collection of concepts, beliefs, values and normative principles supported by material resources. The purpose of the ISDM is to help a development group successfully change object systems, that is to perceive, generate, assess, control, and to carry out change actions in them.   (Lyytinen, 1987, p. 9)

Thus if we are to seek to apply 'fitness for purpose' criteria of quality to both the functioning IS and the development process itself, a very wide range of features requires attention. Furthermore the link between the system and the process must be overt and intimate. Many criticisms of the encompassing methods developed since the early 1980s arise from such methods failing to concentrate on issues outside a relatively restricted section of the technological context. This inevitably leads to systems that are seen from a predominantly rationalistic perspective: systems whose objective is the ever more efficient 'processing and storing of signs in some material carrier' (Lyytinen, 1987, p. 11). Quality then becomes simply a matter of increasing this efficiency.

Accepting that this is an important but severely limited position necessitates introducing non-technical (linguistic and organizational) concerns. This widens the discussion to incorporate the pivotal issues of effectiveness, responsibility, organizational and social context and pressures, power and authority, and so on. Standards can have only a limited role in this complexity, but that is not to deny their importance. An IS has to be regarded not as an isolated product, but as an intrinsic component of its respective environment. Similarly an ISDM has to be assessed in terms of its ability to facilitate rigorous and critical consideration of these issues.

INTERVENING USERS AND QUALITY HORIZONS

Developing from this discussion of IS and ISDM, it is useful to introduce the concepts of *intervening users* and *quality horizons*.

Undermining the manufacturing analogy evoked by the term IS *construction*, there is far more involved in IS development than assembly and delivery of a finished product (however complicated and diverse that might be). A vast range of intervening products are developed, many of them for immediate consumption or refinement by other groups of systems developers.

The relationship between producer and consumer in IS development is not simply that between developer and eventual user. Each group of intervening users—with perhaps clearly identified skills and responsibilities, or more general, flexible roles—can be considered as consumers or customers. The slogan 'customer first' does not then seem to be such an unambiguous call to improved practice. Should consideration be restricted only to the eventual customers? Will problems arise in meeting their needs and also the needs of intervening customers, particularly if the latter include people with responsibilities not merely linked into the chain of production, but also those who have responsibilities for arbitrating, mediating, and negotiating?

This leads on to the concept of quality horizons, essentially recognizing that people occupying this plethora of roles in the overall process will have differing concerns and priorities, and that these need to be recognized and aligned in order that they reinforce rather than undermine any overall quality initiative. If this is not appreciated the quality process may become either a significant restraint in development, or an incomplete and hence problematic exercise.

It may be pointed out that the current trend is to insist on a quality plan, running in tandem with the technical development, and that this should ensure that these divergences (and possible conflicts) are taken into account. Although they do indeed represent an advance in starting to articulate these issues, in most cases there is not sufficient realization of the complexities involved.

We can define a quality horizon as follows:

A quality horizon derives from a particular interest, and applies to a specific context. It will encompass a limited range of tasks or activities contributing to a relatively immediate goal, possibly leading to a more remote or pervasive objective. It will avoid any nebulous concept of 'quality in general', by concentrating on clearly stated and understood completion criteria related to the tasks and aims at hand.

GROWING AND CULTIVATING INFORMATION SYSTEMS

Many of these aspects come into focus if, following Brooks (1986) concerning software, IS are seen as *grown* rather than built. This aligns nicely with the maturity metaphors discussed in the previous chapter, although the overall effect may be to make these issues become even more complex. If this cultivating perspective is adopted, there is less demarcation between constructors and users, in a fashion similar to that adopted by soft systems advocates, whereby everyone involved in the IS context is implicated in its progress.

There is no permitted detachment and disinterestedness on the part of those who might otherwise see their role as delivering a product that others will operate and maintain. On the contrary, the issues that arise around any such system are not seen as fixed and resolvable at an instant. Instead there will be an unremitting cycle of investigation, assessment of priorities, decisions to act to change or persevere with the existing system, and so on.

The demarcation between what are commonly thought of as users and IS professionals begins to breakdown as the processes of systems use and systems development coincide. This blurring of distinctions demands a very clear set of discriminations between quality horizons. Precisely because the situation is not directly that of supplier and customer, oriented around a single point of exchange, the concept of some form of deliverable pertinent at each and every key stage is essential.

There has to be a guiding set of distinct but complementary objectives, and this framework can in part be provided by the idea of groupings of *IS products*, provided that there is sufficient understanding of the manifold features encompassed by this concept.

IS PRODUCTS

Although an IS is sometimes described as a product or commodity, this is misleading. An IS is a product *hierarchy*, consisting of a range of real and virtual products based around the component hardware and software. Each of these products will have its own sphere of quality issues, but there may also be an emergent range of issues that do not relate directly to a specific deliverable. Perhaps the phrase 'virtual quality' needs to be introduced?

This extended view of products qualifies Cargill's distinction between product and process standards when applied to the entire IS area. There is no single IS process, neither is there a distinct set of IS products. It is always going to be easier to apply measurement or assessment to products than it is to processes. But does that mean that only product standards can apply to IS development?

Products or deliverables certainly appear to provide a more tangible focus for quality or other assessment programmes, and the idea of IS products or software products permits a far deeper view of how quality can be incorporated, and standards applied. Whereas the 1960s concept of a software product may have included not much more than the code itself, it would now be expected to involve a range of products extending from initial documentation and decision records, through a full spectrum of delivered items concerning operation, training, and managing the system itself. This is a considerably more sophisticated view of IS products. But it is essentially a static hierarchy, encapsulating the system at an instant.

This is still not the entire picture, however, since the hierarchy extends in another direction which is dynamic. In this sense it includes consideration of deliverables within the timeframe of the development process itself, and it is here that the process aspects come into focus. This involves introducing the distinctions between what will be termed *interim*, *intermediate*, and *component* products. (Further examples of each can be found in the discussion of the SSADM standard in Chapters 5 and 6.)

Interim products are those that are completed at some point of development, but are then consumed—subsumed or assimilated—in the development of further products. Thus many cross-reference products (matrices) would be included in this category.

Intermediate products are those that, although delivered at specified points in development, are further transformed at subsequent stages. This transformation is part of the expected course of development, and not simply as a result of change or discovery of error. An intermediate product will then be a designated variant of some more general product (e.g. in SSADM logical and normalized variants of a logical data model).

Finally component products are those that are delivered fit for use as part of the functioning information system; in many cases these may be 'finished' variants of earlier intermediate products.

Again these discriminations initially assume that the construction model of IS development applies. The threefold view of products implies a distinction being made in the application of quality diagnostics and standards as applied to each category. Thus models such as Boehm's (1978) or McCall's (1979) can be seen as applying most readily to component products, since many of the features they mention—usability, reliability, etc.—have most relevance here. (Although these concepts can be expanded to take into account other aspects, particularly when the growing of an information system is used as a perspective.) This is mostly caused by the derivation of such approaches from an emphasis on the delivered software.

This is an important basis, and is motivated by the need to understand and assess the performing software. With an enlarged scope and vision there is no intrinsic reason why such features should not also be at least as applicable to all types of product. Thus usability, reliability, and so on would have to be clearly related to the specific purpose of a particular product—interim, intermediate, or component.

When one moves away from the construction view of development, to an evolutionary perspective, the distinctions between the three forms of product appear less distinct. Far from suggesting that the categories should be allowed to collapse into a single amorphous collection of products, it should be stressed that there is perhaps greater need to reinforce the distinctions—although it may be necessary to qualify the designation of a deliverable as an intermediate or a component product. Perhaps all products should be identified as interim, intermediate, or component but only with respect to a specified configuration: this is not dissimilar to current views of best practice.

The evolutionary view of IS development highlights the service element of a system. An IS must provide a service, and the quality of this service provision is an aspect that is often overlooked or placed in a secondary category. If systems are thought of as growing and evolving, then the critical point cannot be conceived in terms of product handover, but rather the point at which some form of service provision commences. Configurations can then be located against this point.

SOME EXAMPLES OF IS QUALITY STANDARDS

The application of this threefold range of complexities in the IS realm can be clarified by considering some of the current quality and standards perspectives. For the purposes of this discussion this is not an attempt to offer anything more than a description of the main features of the selected approaches. In particular it is important to recognize how quality issues might be approached, and how different perspectives define and constrain their own range of application, how well they cope with their own defined range, and whether they can be extended to other aspects.

The examples selected here are TickIT, SPICE, and Quantum. These represent some of the most visible and firmly promoted initiatives in the IS standards and quality arena. They also represent a related set of initiatives promoted by UK agencies with a view to nurturing quality and standards in UK systems, and in the case of SPICE extending to the international arena. The ensuing discussion of these approaches aims to illustrate some of the key features that are common to them all, or in which they differ, in particular drawing attention to their main characteristics, and offering a basis for consolidated progress on a wide range of quality issues.

A brief description is given of each, including the development of the approach and its relationship to standards and earlier initiatives. The main assumptions are outlined, particularly those relating to the lifecycle or process models involved in development, and whether the focus is on the software product or the more diverse IS perspective.

TickIT

The DTI's TickIT scheme is outlined in the *TickIT Guide to Software Quality Management System Construction and Certification*, developed from the generic international quality standard ISO9001/EN29001/BS5750 Part 1 (TickIT, 1992). The scheme consists of an outline document backed by certification schemes performed by accredited auditors, and was created following the completion of two DTI-funded reports (Logica, 1988; Price Waterhouse, 1988) which recommended that 'authoritative guidance material was required to assist Quality Management System (QMS) implementors in relating generic ISO9001 requirements to specific software QMS procedures' (TickIT, 1992, p. 3). It also aims to assist purchasers of software in identifying and establishing their role in ensuring that quality software is developed and delivered.

The generic ISO9001 standard, 'Quality Systems—Model for Quality Assurance in Design/Development, Production, Installation and Servicing' (part of the family of standards in the ISO9000 series), was drafted within an engineering context best suited to conventional manufacturing (Wernham, 1991). Since its initial publication in 1987, the ISO has formally recognized that software is different from other forms of industrial products, both in its nature and the process of its production. ISO9000-3 deals specifically with the application of ISO9001 to the development, supply, and maintenance of software (*TickItNews*, Issue 2, May 1992, p. 6). TickIT was developed specifically to apply the lessons of ISO9001 to software production, and now specifically incorporates ISO9000-3.

The main information about the scheme is the reference guide. This does not offer great details of the practical issues concerned with QMS implementation, rather it offers a generic approach, and does not address any of the problems likely to be caused by employment of a particular development philosophy. Training is treated similarly, identified as an area that requires attention but with insufficient detail of the likely problems. It does, however, identify the need for cultural change, but the means by which this is to be achieved are not specified.

Technical issues such as metrics are also identified in this manner. While this may be acceptable for some issues, the application of metrics is a difficult task fraught with dangers and not to be taken lightly. The managerial problems of dealing with metrics are not touched upon at all, despite the fact that measurement of performance is always one of the hardest elements in the introduction of QMS.

Since TickIT aims to offer guidance for the establishment of generic models of software QMS, it does not specify a particular process model. It would, however, be reasonable to state that TickIT guidelines apply most readily to the 'V' process model, as this model provides a basis for the quality control elements given in the guide (TickIT, 1992, p. 82). Other process models could be employed, but perhaps establishing the location of principal QMS activities would not be as simple an operation.

TickIT focuses on software (TickIt, 1992, p. 14) and as such it only applies to a limited range of the full scope of IS issues. Its main reference apart from software is the hardware within which the former operates. It sees software as a product, while a QMS is 'the enabling mechanism which coordinates and controls the functions needed to achieve the required quality of product or service as economically as possible' (TickIt, 1992, p. 34). In effect it sees the QMS as a component of the management of the software development process.

In terms of its range of application, the TickIT authors state that 'the nature of software is such that it is necessary to improve the (development) process to effect an improvement in software quality' (TickIT, 1992, p. 36). This is adequate provided one takes a very wide view of development to include both the product, in the widest sense of the term when considering the information system, as well as the service provided. Unfortunately these points are not made sufficiently explicit, and even a careful reader would assume that a fairly limited view of software construction was meant.

It could be argued that as TickIT is based on the standardized definition of quality, 'the totality of features and characteristics of a product or service that bears on its ability to satisfy stated or implied needs' (ISO8402, 1986), it includes a service view of software development. But service appears only in the form of servicing the product and not in terms of the service provided to the user/purchaser.

The service element regarding IS has been described as 'provided by the designers who must be competent for the design functions they perform' (Slater, 1991). This is the view that pervades TickIT, but IS service provision should be viewed as the ability to meet requirements, not at a single instant, but over an extended period including the life of the product/service.

In terms of application across a wide range of quality issues, TickIT has a number of strengths. As a guide to the application of ISO9001 to software development it emphasizes the fact that software has different character-istics from other products, not only in terms of the end result but also the method by which this is produced. The formal recognition of this in itself is a good thing. It also serves to highlight the value of co-operation between the supplier and the purchaser, and charges both with the responsibility to ensure that the software conforms to the agreed specification, a concept that has been sadly lacking in the software industry but well appreciated in other industries. It provides a basis for implementation of a software QMS, lacking slightly in detail, but highlighting the relevant areas nevertheless.

The auditors' guide (TickIt, 1992, Part 5) is also very useful to the QMS implementor as it gives a view of the QMS from the standpoint of accreditation requirements, i.e. how will the QMS be audited and what considerations will be included.

Perhaps TickIT's main role to date has been in its provision of a recognized standard. It is not restricted to the UK, but is also compatible with European requirements for accredited QMS; and schemes based on TickIT are being implemented across the globe. This allows companies to use certification as an international marketing device. While in the past this has often been the sole reason for achieving accreditation to a recognized standard, it is now becoming more common to hear of companies implementing TickIT-style QMS in order to improve their own overall performance.

TickIT thus offers a useful first stage in quality programmes. But can it be extended into further stages? The implementation of a QMS is seen as an initial step towards total quality management (TQM). TickIT specifically refers to 'The TQM Improvement Model' (TickIT, 1992, p. 9), seeing a QMS as relating to an organization at a specific instant which can then provide the vehicle for continuous improvement. It is through this vehicle that the three driving forces of TQM can operate: management commitment for improvement; motivation for improvement; measurements for improvement.

Implementation of a QMS also has a role to play in furthering the maturity of an organization's software development process, and thus TickIT is also related to the Software Engineering Institute's (SEI) Capability Maturity Model (CMM). Achieving the QMS objective, of ensuring the product is produced under controlled and monitored conditions, should enable software developers to establish themselves on level 3 (defined) of the SEI's CMM, if fully and effectively implemented. Unfortunately this would only be true in the case of the most thorough and ideal QMS. More typically a developer following TickIT would probably move towards level 2 (repeatable) on the five-level scale.

The guide itself places QMS as a central, but initial, element in TQM, yet often accreditation to the standard is seen as the summit of a company's quality achievement. TickIT was recently described as the 'UK's first quality award for the software industry' ('Heseltine stamps TickIT', *Computing*, 19 November, 1992, p. 4): the term 'first' should be understood in the sense of both 'original' and 'initial'. In this way TickIT should be situated in the overall quality approach to IS so that developers and purchasers are able to see how far QMS implementation amplifies quality initiatives; and how much more there is still to be included.

Essentially generic standards 'represent minimum not maximum best practice within any one sector' (TickIT, 1992, p. 8), and therefore the standard should be treated as a minimum, albeit crucial, level of achievement. TickIT should not be seen as a quality end-point when in reality it is merely the first step on the quality trail. Moreover achievement of TickIT does not necessarily signify a commitment to continuous improvement, although this is often taken for granted. And it most certainly is not the full answer to quality in terms of software, and even less so to IS. In any case people are becoming more wary (realistic) with regard to standards, understanding that compliance with a standard does not ensure a quality product.

SPICE

When the UK Ministry of Defence became concerned to raise the quality of the software it purchased, it initiated an investigative study into methods used to assess the capability of software suppliers to fulfil needs as perceived by major procurement organizations. This was published under the name ImproveIT (1991). The resulting interest shown by other major software procurers and software suppliers led to a further phase of activity to extend the study. This arose from ImproveIT's providing a means of assessment to aid process improvement in general.

ImproveIT afforded a framework in which work could progress on standardization, scheme development and investigation, technology transfer, and supporting activities on an international, European, and regional basis. The project, renamed SPICE, has now progressed to the international arena with a view to developing a set of Software Process Assessment Standards. The ISO, in the form of the relevant subcommittee with responsibility for standards in software engineering, accepted the study and proposed a new ISO project to develop a suite of standards on software process assessment.

During these developments wide support has been gained for a software assessment scheme that is in the public domain, widely recognized, and preferably backed by an international standard. Organizations already using or developing such schemes have also expressed their support and committed themselves to provide resources to its development.

The requirements for a Software Process Assessment (SPA) standard, given in the ISO report, state that the standard shall 'not presume specific organizational structures, management philosophies, software lifecycle models, software technologies or software development tools'. In effect this standard will provide a guide that will define the high-level activities, goals and criteria required by good software engineering practice.

The guide will not describe how these activities are implemented but only what is required, thereby exemplifying Cargill's category of the conceptual/process standard. In order to implement these practices, application- or sector-specific guides may be needed which will provide profiles of capability and guidance on how to use them. This will enable generation of process profiles for application- or sector-specific comparison. Thus the SPA standard will be independent of any process model, but will recognize that guidance will be needed to aid implementation. Presumably the implementation sections may need regular updating, with the overall conceptual model remaining fairly static once in place.

Like TickIT, the goal of the project is to improve the quality of software produced. It is therefore similarly limited in its applicability to ISD. Process assessment is based on the premise that 'the quality of software products is largely determined by the quality of the processes that produce them'. This is only a slight expansion on TickIT, which made software quality entirely dependent upon the process. But it still does not take into account that IS consist of more than just software, and that IS quality is dependent upon a wide understanding of the term 'product', as well as of the ISD process, and service provision.

The overall SPA proposal is to develop 'a standard for software process assessment incorporating the best features of existing software assessment methods and extending the concepts through the explicit recognition of the individual business needs of an organization and the measurement of the effectiveness of processes in achieving their goals'. This does allow inclusion of a customer view, but only if the organization sees this as a business goal. The concepts of intervening users and quality horizons would not fit easily into this perspective. SPICE seems reliant upon a more elementary supplier/consumer (procurer) model.

The IT industry has often tended to restrict the customer viewpoint to ensuring that the product meets its requirements. Acceptance of SPICE objectives will allow the customer viewpoint to be widened to include consideration of the ability of the supplier to produce the desired product. But this should be extended still further to include the ability of the supplier to supply a service over time, with all the connotations of 'service' that other industries have already accepted. The study report does mention a 'service process improvement model' and 'service delivery processes', but no detailed explanation of these is given.

SPICE assumes that successful completion of key processes will achieve a goal which itself relates directly to a business need or objective. While this may be of some use to the project initiator and software developer, it does not provide much for a large range of IS users. The IS user would surely rather see key features measured in terms of how successfully they meet user objectives, both project oriented and less focused attributes. This raises the question of the best use for an assessment method that does not evaluate a supplier in terms of the quality of its product, but rather in terms of meeting its own goals at both a project and an organizational level.

Perhaps the best way of forming an interim assessment of what is still mostly a proposal is to contrast SPICE with TickIT. SPICE represents an improvement on TickIT in terms of its range of application, but still sees process improvement as the main means of improving software quality. It does afford a basis for an assessment of process maturity, and aims at enabling suppliers to gauge their position in relation to others once a common basis for comparison has been established. It should also facilitate assessment of suppliers by prospective customers. The project could be extended to cover service issues if a suitable means of assessment could be found. Perhaps this will be brought in at a later date.

Quantum

Quantum was a DTI-commissioned study on the 'feasibility of a measurement-based framework for assurance of software quality' (Quantum, 1992). The study was based on the premise that the quality of software products and development processes could be enormously improved through measurement. The study addressed the feasibility of a measurement-based framework that could be applied to achieve this result.

The conclusion was that such a framework was not only feasible but would be well received in the IT industry, by both software purchasers and suppliers. Again drawing on the process maturity model, the eventual framework must encapsulate the issues of process maturity, and be derived from a programme of research and technology transfer. A further suggestion was the creation of a Software Measurement Laboratory to provide a range of measurement services to industry.

The framework itself was expected to address issues of metrics and standards, among others, for a range of domains, e.g. security-critical systems, CASE tools, or specific methods. Some of these aspects were generic and some domain specific (Quantum, 1992, p. 15). The full range of 'items' was given as follows:

1. Standard definition and terms.
2. Definitions of measurements for quality attributes.
3. Procedures and techniques for making standard measurements.
4. Tools supporting the use of measurements at various points on the maturity scale.
5. Public models capturing relationships between various quality attributes.
6. Calibrations of such models.
7. Empirically derived benchmark data, for comparison.
8. A handbook and a directory giving guidance on how to use the framework.
9. Training materials and courses.
10. Practitioner qualifications in the application of software quality measurement.
11. Accredited training organizations.

12. Accredited third-party evaluation organizations.
13. Guidance on how to extend the framework.

The study suggested that a programme of research should be undertaken to establish the validity and suitability of the framework and to supply empirical data from experimentation (Quantum, 1992, p. 19). It also sought to direct initial research towards administrative systems based on database systems, using SSADM and employing COBOL, C and SQL as target languages (Quantum, 1992, p. 19). This was suggested on the basis that research should be directed towards the most common forms of software activity in the UK.

One of the perceived benefits of a measurement-based framework is that it would allow developers to decide whether a particular process or method would bring the required improvements they expected (Quantum, 1992, p. 28). To do this, methodologies, techniques, etc., all need to be measured in similar situations, allowing for project size, duration, staff skills, and so on. Also developers must be allowed the possibility of comparing their own processes against industry norms, thereby identifying areas for improvement.

In addition to this, the metrics programme needs to alert developers and customers to general areas of concern, providing sufficient significance could be attached to the measures themselves. This is no trivial matter. The Quantum authors offer the following example together with an associated query: 'we find that 35% of post-delivery failures occurred in step 1.5 of SSADM, is this good or bad?' (Quantum, 1992, p. 5).

In common with SPICE, Quantum refers to the SEI-CMM, and the anticipated ISO-CMM, maturity model (Quantum, 1992, p. 24). The overall framework will need to be supported by a self-sustaining infrastructure that will include the above features and be operated by the software community. As with ImproveIT and TickIT, Quantum derives from a limited conception of ISD as it applies only to the software product and its development process. Again this falls short of the three views of IS quality, i.e. product, process, and service.

The framework will have to address the definition and creation of standards that will support measurement-based evaluation of software quality, and will also have to consider procedures to measure and compare various software quality attributes. These will have to cover both the software product and the development process, from both supplier and customer perspectives.

The main problem with initiatives such as Quantum is that both the software product and the development process are difficult to measure. Quality attributes such as ease of use, cost, and functionality may be measured (or at least compared) relatively easily. Maintainability may have to be represented by substitutes such as measures of complexity or the availability of design documentation.

Difficulties also arise in understanding what to measure and how to measure it. Having once established a range of measurements, it may be difficult to understand the relative importance of different measures. In addition the construction metaphor for software systems contributes to this misplaced reliance on measurements.

These apart, Quantum appears to offer a step in the right direction. Objective measurement of software process capability, maturity, and the software product itself are all highly commendable objectives. The project also sought to consolidate various initiatives currently available in the software community, and position them relative to each other (Quantum, 1992, p. 18).

Different forms of measurement are recognized, and the assumption is that measurements that aid the achievement of control and predictability of the software process must be applied before measurements which, for example, support improvement in reliability or productivity.

The Quantum approach is very far reaching. It could be argued that it represents the ultimate quality initiative. On the other hand, its objectives could be viewed as so fanciful that it is unlikely ever to achieve a fraction of its aims. The latter view seems to be predominating, as little more has been heard about the project since publication of the initial report in 1992.

PROCESS MATURITY

The three schemes described above all draw on the concept of process maturity mentioned in the earlier chapters; TickIt implicitly, the other two explicitly.

The software process maturity model is not itself a standard, but a framework within which a whole range of activities can be located and contrasted. Intelligent use of the concepts and the supporting material such as the SPMM assessment questionnaire, offer a useful diagnostic tool—and moreover one that has been partially calibrated on a wide scale. It is, therefore, a useful foundation for any quality programme, but particularly relevant to an initiative such as Quantum which seeks to establish a generally recognized and widely applicable measure.

More importantly the concept of capability assessment has caught the imagination of those involved in procurement of IS/IT. This will almost certainly ensure that suppliers have to gain accreditation in line with some form of the model. This is already beginning to happen, with suppliers claiming 'level 5 on CMM', and with customers demanding a minimum level 3 rating from those tendering for certain contracts.

Maturity has become the basis for a range of software quality initiatives such as SPICE and Quantum because it can be used to indicate a whole range of aspects of a supplier organization. It also promises an objective premise for such judgements, particularly as envisaged by the Quantum report.

One main criticism of SPMM and the like is that it focuses primarily on the development process, and makes little attempt to cover areas such as acceptance, replication, delivery, and installation, which even TickIT identifies. Furthermore it is assumed that all supplier companies need to be at level 5, but this is hardly necessary. Indicators of maturity must be tempered with the business objectives and needs of the system. This is in part the reasoning behind SPICE and its use of company objectives along with the maturity model to evaluate and improve process maturity.

The concept of organizational maturity is, however, a powerful one. It clarifies many of the current debates on IS quality and standards, since it affirms that standards have an important yet limited role to play in overall improvement programmes. In fact the principles of maturity can be applied to the development of standards themselves in the sense that early standards have to be applied for basic features such as safety, compatibility, and customer confidence (*consistent and predictable expectation*). Once this basis is in place, standards in the form of *qualitative comparisons* and *desired objectives* can be defined and used to generate not merely a predictable context for development, but qualitatively improved performance all round.

The transition from abstract quality standards, to the appearance of BS5750 and TickIT represents the first stage of such a progression. The ambitions behind SPICE and Quantum are to extend this basis into the realms of qualitative comparison and desired objective. But at present they are not sufficiently developed or supported to offer practical guidance on such aspects of IS development, or even simply on software development.

It must at present be concluded that the IS/SE standards world remains insufficiently mature to generate and appreciate fully developed quality standards and embodiments of best practice. The present need is for base standards of the sort indicated in the Appendix, standards that will promote and support consistent and predictable expectations for both suppliers and customers. Some of the existing IT standards already do this at the level of the technology. In order to expand this foundation, standards must be developed that address the IS itself in a similar fashion: the development of the standard for SSADM exemplifies an early and tentative advance in this progression.

5

THE DEVELOPMENT OF THE SSADM STANDARD—PART I: FROM INCEPTION TO PREPARATION OF THE DRAFT FOR PUBLIC COMMENT

SSADM—A PUBLIC SECTOR 'STANDARD'

SSADM first came into existence in the early 1980s, prompted by the requirement for a standard (i.e. exemplary or archetypal) approach to control and constrain those supplying IS products to the UK government sector.

Version 2, dating from the mid-1980s, stressed the need for a 'standard approach' to integrate the structure, procedures, and documentation associated with an IS development project. This would lessen 'the risk of wasting resources', increase the productivity of development staff, and allow effective user intervention and review (SSADM, 1985, Introduction).

In Cargill's (1989) sense of the term as providing the basis for a common interchange, SSADM was always destined to act as a standard. To this end early versions were tightly focused and prescriptive: that is, were an implementation/process standard. These early versions sought to be constrained and constraining, providing users with a readily understand-able and applicable structure that could be imposed on development projects in order to permit users some degree of comprehension and control: a standard in the sense of a consistent and predictable expectation.

SSADM was a revised and refocused variant of an existing method (LSDM). It was selected after fairly exhaustive surveys of the wide variety of available methods, and was designed to provide a firm and stable foundation in an area of change and potentially costly confusion. The main objective for SSADM was to act as a limitation and pressure on systems development, since a significant amount of resource expended on such developments was wasted—most frequently a result of imprecise specification of requirements, and lack of proper control of the project by users in the period from agreeing the specification to delivery of the finished system. This was not in any way unique to the procurement of UK public sector systems. It was a commonplace for all systems and all contexts, but occurred on a larger and more visible scale in the context of government expenditure and services.

CLARIFYING TERMINOLOGY

Before proceeding any further on the topic of methods and methodologies, some of the terminology must be clarified. Strictly speaking the use of the term *methodology* applies to the study and justification of approaches to a particular field of interest or knowledge. A *method*, on the other hand, is a statement defining the way in which some task is to be achieved.

For a variety of reasons the terms have become used almost synonymously with regard to IS approaches. This is only partly explained by linguistic misuse, which is a common feature of the IS/IT environment. On the other hand, there is the need to justify any approach to IS development, rather than simply to outline the tasks and techniques: *every method has to provide its own methodology*.

For the purposes of this discussion the following definitions will be assumed:

- *Modelling facilities*—provide abstraction mechanisms expressed in some syntactically constrained notation.
- *Techniques*—outline and guide the construction and manipulation of the models/abstractions.
- *Methods*—detail the process of applying techniques associated with a model to a context.
- *Methodologies*—explain the basis for the combination and synthesis of a variety of models through an amalgamation of different methods.
- *Tools*—may support any of the aspects of the above.

This gives some basis for a distinct terminology, but does not offer a clear separation of method from methodology. This is not really a problem, and does reflect the point made earlier that any IS method has not only to detail the processes and procedures, but also to justify their inclusion and combination.

Although the 'M' of SSADM denotes *method*, SSADM is also a methodology in the sense of the term defined above. All IS methods have this dual nature, and in this context the term 'method' will be used to mean both method and methodology as defined above, unless an explicit point needs to be made with regard to only one of the aspects.

LET A THOUSAND METHODS BLOOM

In the 1970s, when IS methods first appeared, there was a good deal of scepticism regarding their value, particularly those that aimed to cover a large proportion of the IS lifecycle. Some of this scepticism was overcome through experience; some simply by the force of the market demand: if clients demanded expertise in a particular method as a condition of tendering for a contract, then that expertise would have to be supplied.

Whatever the balance between the two forces of scepticism and client demand, by the mid-1980s several hundred methodologies had blossomed, and the argument for their effectiveness appeared to have been won. But the early methods, including SSADM (in Version 2 by this time), were now seen as too restrictive, and the necessity for a more expansive version of SSADM became pressing. This demand was in part the result of the increasing sophistication of alternative methods, together with the contexts and uses to which they were being put, and in part also because the SSADM user community was growing in non-government, commercial sectors.

In addition the late 1970s and early 1980s witnessed the transition from old-style *data processing* to the development of *information systems* activities. Data processing had been regarded as a series of operations completed behind closed doors between various peculiar forms of approved and compatible technology, protected by technically proficient experts. Non-specialists did not need to concern themselves with the intricacies; existing organizational procedures were unaffected, except in so far as some aspects were now automated or performed faster.

This blissful state of ignorance could no longer be maintained once the era of the 'IS' dawned. In this phase the technology started to impinge increasingly on mundane and everyday tasks and issues. It was no longer a case of liking or loathing the technology; it was more a case of both the technology and tasks it was designed to support becoming components of a wider *system*. Since the components had to interact, indifference was not a feasible stance.

This is another aspect of Jackson's argument concerning organizational technological maturity (see Chapter 3). The development came about for a variety of reasons linked both to technological advance (e.g. the advent of the PC), new economies of scale (falling prices of hardware, larger markets for packaged software, etc.) and encroachment of technology into an increasingly wide domain of organizational activities (from invoicing and order processing to cheque clearing, financial modelling, and so on).

Systems were becoming more complex, interfacing with other systems, and expanding in scope. Any methods concerned with guiding and enhancing the development of such systems had to mature and evolve at least as much as the target systems themselves. Thus new or enhanced methods arose for the development of *information systems*, stressing the organizational and strategic features of such systems. Some also explicitly encompassed human interface and usability issues, with, for instance, enlarged emphasis on requirements capture through prototyping. This is what is meant by the 'increasing sophistication' of methods alluded to above.

Developments in SSADM reflected some of these changes, and in 1986 SSADM Version 3 was launched. It differed from Version 2 in its format and detail, but more crucially it emerged from the confines of the government sector to become a self-proclaimed *open*, non-proprietorial method.

In this the method was unique, since no restrictions were placed on its use, and no licence was required to apply the method. But control of the method was retained by the UK government through the CCTA (originally the Central Computer and Telecommunications Agency, now simply CCTA: The Government Centre for Information Systems), and more directly the Design Authority Board (DAB). It thus differed from proprietary methods such as Yourdon or Information Engineering (IE), which required a form of user licence; and also from other public sector methods such as the French government sponsored MERISE, which was allowed to evolve in a less restricted fashion and soon existed in several (potentially incompatible) versions.

The reasoning behind the development of a non-proprietorial, yet centrally controlled SSADM was that everything possible should be done to encourage the growth and application of the method—both within public and private sectors—but that the method itself must be protected from uncontrolled change and multiple variants. This cuts across Gabel's categories, since SSADM became virtually a public standard, but at the same time provided the basis for a network of products—specifically training courses, CASE tools, and development practices.

Soon after the launch of Version 3, the SSADM Users Group (UG) was established as the prime forum for non-government users of the method. (Government users were not discouraged from membership of the group at this time, but they already had their own, internal SSADM group. By the late 1980s this latter group merged with the UG. In 1992 the SSADM UG was renamed the International SSADM Users Group.) This expansion, both of the method and of the user-base, added to the stature of the method, and although there were many areas in which Version 3 was, if not deficient as such, certainly weak in comparison with alternative approaches, the extent of its use and acceptance counterbalanced these. This status was also enhanced by associated projects such as the Tools Certification Scheme and the Certificate of Proficiency.

The CCTA, controllers of SSADM, could claim by the latter half of the 1980s that SSADM not only offered a method for systems development, but also provided a series of support mechanisms for staff training and development, tool support, and additional guidelines. Rather than presenting SSADM as simply another alternative in the methods marketplace, the developments around Version 3 resulted in a foundation for many types of organization to develop a coherent and pragmatic methods strategy. This also meant that the emergence of quality initiatives such as TickIT could be seen as representing an enhancement of existing methods strategies.

METHODS—CURE OR AILMENT?

By the late 1980s, however, the overall image of structured methods was somewhat tarnished. The 1980s had seen a flourishing of information systems development methodologies (ISDMs) aimed specifically, and vociferously, at resolving a host of problems associated with the IS development process. In particular these methodologies sought to enhance system delivery, increase productivity, auditability, user acceptance, verifiability, and validity, while decreasing cost, maintenance, and schedule. Yet by the late 1980s some critics were pointing to the deficiencies of the ISDMs themselves as contributors in part to the IS malaise. The cure was proving almost as debilitating as the sickness.

One key reason for this emanated from what might be termed the temporal paradox between a system and its specification in the terms required within a methodological framework. Systems are dynamic, and constantly changing. Methodologies, used unimaginatively, impose an unyielding format and timescale for systems development. Almost all of them offer a path from requirements to implementation which consists of a fairly strict sequence of diverse activities, production of deliverables, and quality decision points which are mandatory or critical to the totality of the final product and any intermediate products.

In this way methodologies resemble steamrollers advancing slowly but irresistibly, reducing every obstacle to a single dimension (as near as possible), obscuring or ignoring aspects that cannot be encompassed. This would not be particularly unsatisfactory if the target context was static, the specification, or requirements frozen. But this is not the case. The capture of requirements in the first, and subsequent instances is never adequate. Moreover the requirements change as the development proceeds. Using a steamroller to apprehend so animated an object is hardly the most effective application of technology to a problem domain.

It might be argued that many methodologies in their later versions did and do attempt to resolve these contradictions. Thus it could be claimed that the temporal imbalance has been mediated through associations with panaceas such as fourth-generation languages or prototyping, or currently fashionable 'rapid' development approaches. But these remedies are rarely more than a tinkering with the methodologies themselves, rather than substantive attempts to create a new strategy to serve as a resolution to the problem. The result is that these enhancements deal with the symptoms at a superficial level, rather than effecting a more profound solution.

In many respects this is not surprising since the most promising strategy for overcoming these problems would have to involve an attempt to define the IS domain in such a way that the full gamut of methods, models, techniques, tools, and so on could be located against such a characterization and hence related to each other. (The current Euromethod project, funded by the EU, is an attempt to offer this sort of framework, but it is slanted heavily towards the procurement aspects of IS. It remains to be seen how useful it will be in the general IS area.) Such a project extends well beyond the confines of a single methodology, particularly since most of the latter are premised on a specific segment of a waterfall-like process model.

Staunch defenders of specific structured methods might point to the commonly accepted distinction between *data structure* and *process*, the key to most structured methods, as a resolution of the paradox of a firm but flexible basis for a system. The data structure is meant to offer a stable system basis which, if correctly specified, can provide a firm foundation capable of supporting complex and changing requirements. The limitations of this assertion, and of the methodologies themselves, however, become apparent when the focus shifts from the immediately conspicuous realm of data processing or even some fairly conventional IS aspects to, for instance, that of complex planning systems or real-time implementations, where the stable component is based on the interactive dynamics of the system.

In fact the arguments advanced by, among others, Mumford and Boehm (1986), indicate that the data/process distinction is questionable even for conventional systems. Mumford's work on her ETHICS approach to systems development demarcates *stable centres* from *adaptive peripheries*: However, there is no simple rule for making the demarcation in general terms, each context will be unique and uniquely developing. Recognition of the respective components is a critical aspect of early phases of the construction of a system.

Boehm, in advancing a spiral model of software development, which can be extended to the IS realm as a whole, considers many similar arguments. For Boehm the development and enhancement process centres on progressive identification of objectives, risks, and alternatives. This may start with a search for a stable basis upon which to build other more dynamic or ambiguous features; but on the other hand, it may be that the most risk-prone features become the centre of attention at the start of a development. (Those tempted to wave the banner of object orientation at this point should be cautious about accepting the universal applicability of object-oriented approaches to IS development—see Bryant and Evans, 1994.)

For the most part structured methods emanate primarily from one concern within the scope of software development: software management. Those elevating management aspects to prime position concentrate on planning, monitoring, and control features of software production on a large scale. For them the major interest is in perfecting the discipline provided by clear objectives, activities, and tasks defined within a well-structured process model or lifecycle approach.

Structured methods build upon this consideration. This is in contrast to those who favour software reliability or productivity as the primary facets. In the former case there is a concentration on the production of error-free code aided by rigorous and formal languages for the development of proof techniques based on mathematical models: discipline develops from well-founded (mathematically based) theory. In the latter case anything that increases productivity in terms of the software is favoured. Since the only tangible measure can be in terms of lines of code, this will lead to encouragement of anything that increases the daily rate per programmer, or enhances each line, i.e. use of ever more powerful computer languages.

Clearly all these three aspects must be combined in any one realistic strategy for systems improvement—and as was argued in the last chapter, the service factor must also be incorporated. The general picture must be a multi-dimensional one, capable of encompassing emphases on management, monitoring, control, productivity, rigour, verification, precision, productivity, service levels, performance; and a whole host of other aspects.

This inherent complexity effectively precludes the possibility of any one method, methodology, or approach providing the basis for guidance for more than a small proportion of systems activities and concerns. For the IS practitioner this post-modern feature of pluralism is embodied in the objective of *methods integration*. Thus any single method must now admit the impossibility of providing a universal panacea; something that, for instance, the world of object-orienteers finds hard to accept.

THE MATURING OF IS METHODS

The history of SSADM is to a large extent a reflection of this maturing of IS methods. The method emerged from the ideas of the 1970s which stressed the importance of mechanisms for decomposing complexity through modularity, e.g. loose coupling and strong cohesion. These ideas, first applied to the level of application program code, soon expanded into the design level, and eventually to the earlier stages of requirements capture, termed 'analysis' in order to distinguish it from the more detailed and implementation-specific 'design'.

The early approaches to structured analysis and design borrowed a good deal from more traditional disciplines, such as O&M and pre-IT systems analysis. Although relatively informal, such procedures were far less haphazard than what had passed for 'design' of computer-based systems previously.

In time a more formal basis was offered in the work of Constantine and Yourdon (1979), among others. This was then supplemented by the emerging methods based around database design, stressing the separation between the logical and the physical, and the insistence on the structuring of data to permit a wide variety of manipulations and queries.

LSDM (the proprietary method of Learmonth and Burchett Management Systems), the basis of SSADM, was initially a modelling method for database applications, and only later became a systems development method. It accomplished this by adding additional views or perspectives to augment the data model. By the time the method was bought-in for developing into SSADM there were three views: data, process, and event. For Version 2 these were termed data structure, information flow, and event; and the three models were respectively Logical Data Structure, Data Flow Diagram, and Entity Life History. Version 2 was still an in-house UK government approach, which had been made mandatory for the procurement of IS. The repository of SSADM expertise and knowledge was the CCTA as part of the latter's general function to supply government departments with advice and guidance on the procurement of computer and communications systems.

In addition, one of CCTA's unintended, unofficial but pivotal roles was to provide the private sector with a steady supply of highly experienced and knowledgeable IS and specifically SSADM practitioners, who quickly established themselves as consultants or founders of IS companies. This accelerated the diffusion of SSADM knowledge into the public sector, and raised the level of interest in SSADM, and it was not long before pressure grew to make the method accessible outside government departments. So what at first sight appears to be a weakening of the SSADM-base, proved to be part of the foundation for its more general use and growth.

Version 3, appearing in 1986, was initially still an in-house method, but was soon placed in the public domain with publication of the manuals by NCC/Blackwell (1987). This coincided with the moves to found the SSADM Users Group. (The Design Authority Board (DAB) too eventually opened up to non-government, non-CCTA representatives, but this happened sometime later.)

These changes in the supporting structure of the method were also accompanied by changes in the content of SSADM. Version 3 had moved some way to accommodate specific issues such as maintenance, prototyping, packaged software, and so on; although the quality and integrity of these optional extras was in many instances well below that of the main components of the method. In any case the general tenor of the method was still prescriptive in the sense that it would provide a stable basis for user, procurer, and supplier expectations and interactions.

The problem was that it was often felt that what was needed was a more flexible and descriptive approach, recognizing that a single method could not cover all developments and details. There was then a pressure to move the method from a prescriptive one to a structure within which a wide variety of approaches and technologies could complement one another. Version 3 did not offer this; perhaps a new version would.

VERSION 4

The methods world, like that of IT and IS in general, does not lend itself to stasis. Version 3, and its associated initiatives, had only a limited productive and useful life. This period was inevitably to be affected by a multitude of developments and changes. The very fact that the UK government had its own method was an influential factor in the development of other methods, and additional techniques to SSADM itself. There were also the rapid advances in technology at this time, particularly in the power and cost of PCs and peripherals—printers and screens—with better definition output, and also the development of CASE tools by way of workbenches, diagram editors, and so on. Taken together this greatly expanded the role and scope of computer-based IS, and also afforded the developers more options and tools.

The following were some of the main pressures influencing SSADM, and other methods, in the late 1980s.

Methods support technology

The development of CASE had been much heralded during the 1980s. To a large extent the target of many CASE products was rather nebulous: 'the software product', or 'systems project'. There were exceptions where the

CASE support was highly focused, and there were other CASE tools that were method specific and method directed. There had been attempts to develop SSADM-specific tools during this period, some of the earlier ones foundering as they could not offer multi-user capabilities. Later the market was simply too complex for the launch of a strictly SSADM CASE tool. The UK government, in the shape of the CCTA, could not compete against the established CASE tool vendors. So eventually the prime initiative moved from product development to product endorsement, directed through the SSADM Research Centre located in Birmingham Polytechnic. Here CASE tool vendors could offer their products as SSADM support tools, either in an SSADM-specific form or as part of a more generic capability.

This interesting, but (in its first embodiment) short-lived, project attempted to produce a series of ratings for CASE tools claiming adherence to and support for Version 3. Suppliers were invited to submit their products for a series of tests, the results of which were synthesized into a final star rating, ranging from 1* (correct diagrammatic syntax) to 4* (full support for all models and the procedures of the method). Such certification was no trivial matter since the potential market was large, and any tool supplier failing to gain a rating could suffer considerable restriction in potential sales.

Up until 1990 a series of products were submitted for testing. The first formal ratings were announced in 1990, with one product gaining the 3* rating, four more 2*, and one with 1*. This proved to be something less significant than might at first appear, since by that time Version 4 was ready and so the Version 3 ratings were somewhat outdated if not devalued. (In addition the product gaining 3* did nothing to prevent its parent organization undergoing severe financial problems thereafter.) The scheme formally ended in 1990 with the advent of Version 4, and the departure of most of the relevant skilled personnel from Birmingham Polytechnic. The Version 4 scheme, controlled through the CCTA itself, is slightly different in its form and content, some aspects of which are still uncertain at the time of writing.

Since the user-base of SSADM was and is so large and significant, suppliers have been keen to substantiate any claim to support SSADM. On the other hand, there are methods other than SSADM that also represent significant market share, and to which suppliers will want to be able to aim their products. Furthermore each supplier will also want to add new features to differentiate their product from competitors.

The CASE market is very risky, costly to enter, and highly competitive; it is also fast moving and replete with questionable claims by suppliers and developers. On the other hand, systems developers and their clients are keen to use any technology that affords faster delivery and more cost-effective systems. Methods such as SSADM cannot simply ignore the developments of CASE. In the private sector one of the dangers is that organizations will become technology driven in their adoption of a particular CASE tool. In the public sector, particularly in the context of the EU, governments cannot be seen to favour one product or supplier over others. As a consequence SSADM had to develop to keep pace with the CASE technology, at the very least guiding the SSADM community around the CASE marketplace; but also replacing the paper-based flavour of the method with a perceptively CASE-enhanced one.

Methods maturity

The idea of a method for systems development has evolved since the 1970s. Not only had the technology changed out of all recognition by the late 1980s (and the associated users' expectations, range of applications, and so on), but also the range, background, and experience of systems developers was markedly different from that of their predecessors. For example, one of the key differences in recent years is that many systems professionals have not previously been full-time programmers, and may never even have written a computer program of any kind. Methods have to reflect this division of labour and variety of expertise.

The changes in methods in the late 1970s and early 1980s reflected an increasing awareness of the scope of systems projects, and the extended range of issues involved at distinct stages of development. Thus problems of feasibility were specifically addressed, techniques designed for incorporation of database concepts and implementations were included, and the specific problems of maintenance and small-scale development—including use of packaged software—were confronted.

The overall resonance of a prescriptive guide to development, which had marked early versions of methods, e.g. SSADM Version 2, was not amended or tempered. In fact it was exacerbated by the addition of these new concerns. This was doubly problematic since it demotivated experienced staff who might feel that there were possible alternatives to a particular method's route, and also offered little guidance for incorporation of new techniques or tools that emerged only after the release date of the current version of the method. For all that, the creators and promulgators of methods protested that their methods were not monolithic and stifling inventions; many users claimed that the methods did indeed constrain development through their prescriptiveness and overwhelmingly detailed dictates. These criticisms proved irresistible by the late 1980s.

Political/social factors and the European Community

By 1990, the anxiously anticipated Version 4 of SSADM was released. The method now was located within a framework of associated activities and concerns, and explicitly positioned within the wider IS lifecycle. Moreover, it was recognized that the role of a method had changed from a set of tightly integrated procedures to a more flexible configuration of techniques and activities, potentially supported (or even in part supplanted) by additional guides or methods. There was, therefore, a core SSADM that could be enhanced and embellished. In order to demonstrate how this could be achieved, the four-volume manual would eventually be supplemented by a series of interface guides.

A key aspect of Version 4 is its proclaimed status as an 'open method'. This has a variety of implications, some better understood than others. One of the main implications is that there are no licences associated with use of SSADM, nor is the CCTA or the DAB concerned with selling, let alone monopolizing, SSADM-related products, tools, or services. On the other hand, the DAB is concerned with control of the method, in order to prevent the preponderance of SSADM clones. The DAB could be said to relate to the method in the role of stewardship rather than as owner or proprietor. In this role, therefore, questions of training, consultancy, tool support, certification, and accreditation arise.

Various schemes derived from Version 3 have been taken into the domain of Version 4, including the ISEB (Information Systems Examination Board, previously the Systems Analysis Examination Board [SAEB]) regime for SSADM instructors, courses, and examinations, and also the Tools Certification Scheme. The openness of the method must not allow the growth of uncoordinated developments resulting in a chaotic mess where no one knows where ultimate responsibility and control reside. One of the prime objectives of the DAB is to prevent this situation arising.

Moreover, overall control of the use of the method has grown in complexity as the user-base has increased, matured, and moved beyond the scope of the UK government sector into the European and international realm. In order to facilitate control and responsible use of SSADM, not only must the practitioners—and suppliers—of SSADM understand the method, but so too must those *procuring*, *acquiring*, and *managing* systems.

In addition, by 1989–90 it was becoming clear that there were likely to be extensive ramifications for IS development, procurement, and acquisition with the advent of the single European market in 1993. The dawning of January 1993 would not quite lead to the possibility of pan-European connectability and compatibility, but it would be the start of a far more open market for the supply of, for instance, IS products and services, with suppliers originating in any of the EC (later EU) member states, responding to invitations to tender (ITTs) with real expectations of gaining business. The presumption that SSADM could remain a 'very British method', and continue to be mandated throughout the public sector would not last beyond 1993.

One anticipated effect of the arrival of the single European market was that announcements of ITTs for public-sector procurement could no longer specify particular products. The inclusion of named products would in most cases breach the relevant directives on freedom of competition across the community. This would apply to 'products' such as SSADM. On the other hand, it appeared that it would be permissible (and even recommended) to quote public standards in ITTs: a key argument to promote a standard for SSADM.

INITIATING THE SSADM STANDARD

These three impulses—control at the point of acquisition; a desire to control the offerings of CASE vendors; and the advent of the single market—were behind the decision to initiate the process of producing a standard for SSADM.

In January 1990 a proposal to establish a group charged with developing a standard for SSADM had been presented to the BSI Committee IST/15 (Software Development and Documentation, later retitled Software Engineering). The overall reaction had been favourable, but further explanation of the 'benefits of a standard' had been requested. By the time the Technical Panel (TP) first met (14 June 1990), the proposal had been accepted, and the first task of the TP was to agree a schedule and programme of work.

The CCTA had initiated the proposal for a standard, and it was at their instigation that the TP had been assembled. The CCTA suggestion was that the standard should consist of part of the (as yet unpublished and unseen) documentation for SSADM Version 4, i.e. a subset of the proposed four-volume manual, plus one extra item. The nominated sections from the manual would include the following:

1. Structural Model—including diagrams and activity descriptions
2. Dictionary—product breakdown structure(s), product descriptions, glossary

And the additional item:

3. Entity Relationship Attribute model of deliverables.

The SSADM standard would be of the 'method for specifying' type of standard (see below):

By providing a standard representation for the terminology, structure and deliverables of SSADM, the standard will be valuable for the specification of contractual requirements and will promote consistency, quality and competition in the supply of services, and products related to SSADM. (extract from the CCTA proposal put to BSI)

Moreover the benefits would accrue around procurement activities, service provision, and user expectation, accreditation, and testing schemes, and promoting competition.

The proposal also noted that, at the time of writing, SSADM was already a *de facto* standard, and that soundings around the SSADM user community had indicated that the time was right for 'a formal definition of the SSADM process and its deliverables'.

The potential benefits of the standard would include the following (all from the CCTA proposal to the BSI, January 1990):

- Promoting quality and consistency.
- Facilitating procurement by providing a formal means of specifying the use of SSADM contractually.
- Helping the provision of services and products by providing a stable specification for suppliers.
- Providing a basis for accreditation and testing schemes.
- Promoting an open and competitive market in IT services.

Although revised in the light of the comments made by the parent committee, the proposal document failed to deal specifically with the problem of the planned scope of the standardization activity. More critically the range of benefits was too wide, unconstrained, and potentially divergent. Rather than concentrating on the method as documented in the manuals, the proposal mentioned 'semi-formal' elements in the SSADM domain, presumably including aspects such as the SAEB (now ISEB) Training Accreditation Scheme and SSADM Research Centre Tools Conformance Scheme. This moved attention away from stating and adhering to a principal objective for producing a standard for SSADM.

Furthermore, one implication of the proposal document was that the standard for SSADM would standardize both the process and the product aspects of the method. This was not a good basis for convening a disparate group of people, representing a wide range of interests, to contribute to standards development.

THE TECHNICAL PANEL

At the inaugural meeting of the TP most of those attending were people invited by the convenor, representing numerous relevant concerns: the CCTA, who supplied the convenor and secretary; the British Computer Society; the SSADM Research Centre at Birmingham Polytechnic; the Ministry of Defence; the SSADM Users Group; BT; IST/15; and other IST/15 panel convenors.

It is worth stressing that in fact anyone who is interested can attend a BSI TP meeting, and it is not necessary to be a representative of an organization or professional body. The only qualification is that any expenditure of effort or resources is not reimbursed by the BSI. (Contribution to standards making is far more a case of persistence than prominence.)

One of the issues that was raised almost immediately concerned the scope of the standardization activity of the group itself. It was agreed that in no way could the TP take on the role of producing a general 'standard for systems development methods'. This might be tempting, but was certain to be a Sisyphean labour given all the interested parties who would be determined to ensure that their particular product fitted within the putative standard. Whatever the content and composition of the resulting standard, it had to be distinctively SSADM—both because it was SSADM specifically that was to be standardized, and because any wider set of demands would prove too difficult and disparate to satisfy.

WHAT TYPE OF STANDARD?

This agreed, there was next the question of the type of standard to be developed. The three-volume BS0 offers a range of different types of standard, essentially based around the object of the standardization activity itself. The options specified in BS0 are as follows:

a) specifications for products or materials: dimensions, performance, safety, etc.; specifications for processes, practices, systems, etc.;
b) methods of measuring, testing, analysing, specifying, etc.;
c) recommendations on product or process applications; codes of practice;
d) terminology, symbols;
e) classification.   (BS0, Part 3, p. 6)

These are each defined (BS0, Part 3, Section 2.1) as follows:

BS specifications lay down requirements to be satisfied by a product, material, process or system, together with the methods by which conformity may be verified.

BS methods formalize ways of doing things.

BS codes of practice recommend good, accepted practice for the accomplishment of a defined task. They are advisory, not intended to provide objective criteria by which compliance may be judged.

BS glossaries define and standardize terminology, often in association with units, symbols and conventions. Classifications have the same status as glossaries; their function is to designate and describe different grades of product or arrange data in an agreed hierarchical order.

The initial proposal had been to produce a standard in the form of a method for specifying. This seemed natural since the aim was to standardize the method: SSADM. But this type of standard was far more difficult to apply to the process of IS development than it might be, say, to a more constrained, straightforward, and less extensive process. (Many quality standards are of the methods for specifying type in that they specify the assessment methods that have to be performed.) It was clear that the sort of standard envisaged had not been developed before; no one had developed a standard for a method of the nature and complexity of SSADM.

In any case there was no clear statement of what aspects of SSADM were to be standardized. SSADM could be considered as a *method*, composed of certain activities grouped into stages, modules, and so on. It could also be considered to be a *set of techniques*, with guidelines on the application of those techniques. Finally it could be seen as a *set of practices* which resulted in the delivery of *products* relevant to the design and delivery of a computer-based information system. There was no reason why it should not be seen as all three, particularly in its role as a method. But it could not be all of these things in a single standard.

In fact there is a very good case to be made for the method to retain all these aspects in a strongly interrelated fashion. But once the topic of developing a standard arises it is not at all obvious which aspects should be standardized. The most obvious solution might appear to be to standardize the whole lot, but this would be to mistake the nature of standards. It is to see standardization as a sort of embalming process, preserving the perfect specimen as a model for others to emulate. But not even the most adamant proponent of SSADM Version 4 would argue for such an elevated status. This then begs the question: 'What parts of SSADM can and should be standardized—products, procedures, techniques (processes)?'

In fact the idea of laying down explicit procedures for implementing SSADM in an IS development context runs counter to the philosophy of Version 4 which explicitly mentions '*maximum flexibility* in techniques and implementation tools' (Version 4, Vol. 1, Introduction, 1-INT-v, italics in original).

Similarly the techniques, or processes, are also unsuitable as candidates for standardization. Some of them are not specific to SSADM (data flow and logical data modelling techniques), and others are clearly derived from other sources (entity life histories).

The crucial point is that the philosophy of Version 4 is specifically *product driven*; progress through the method, and hence through stages of development, is substantiated through delivery and acceptance of agreed and acknowledged outcomes. This should have indicated that the most promising standardization strategy would be built around SSADM-type products. But such a conclusion took rather longer to emerge.

Discussion in the TP meetings initially failed to focus on products in this way, and instead ranged across a wide spectrum of ideas and issues. This was in part because the Version 4 manual itself was specifically addressed to a whole host of groups—practitioners, user managers, trainers, service and product providers, project and technical managers, and IT directorate staff, standards makers, and coordinators ('They will be interested in the Structural Model and the Dictionary', Version 4, F-INT-5), as well as data administrators and information managers and academics. Many of those contributing to the deliberations of the TP represented one or more of these interests. Consequently, as part of the consensual atmosphere surrounding standards making, most of the early attempts at scoping the standard sought to cover most or all of these aspects. (One of the early documents presented to the TP from one of its members detailed an eight-fold classification [1991] ranging across different roles and perspectives in the development process. This can now be seen as a conflation of several distinct facets of standardization. Specifically it combines product, process, and resource considerations and even alludes to notational ones [see Chapter 3]. Perhaps at this point the services of a professional standards maker should have been invoked; unfortunately this did not occur, and a spurious and illusory resolution was effected.)

What was agreed at this stage (late 1990) was that the most uncontroversial and tangible aspect of the application of SSADM was the delivery of SSADM-type products. The existing Version 4 manual listed these as a separate section—the Dictionary, which was specifically mentioned as being of interest to standards makers.

The full range of products specified in the dictionary incorporated more than those directly concerned with the development of IS applications. This is illustrated in Figs 5.1–5.3, owing as much to general principles of project management and quality as to SSADM.

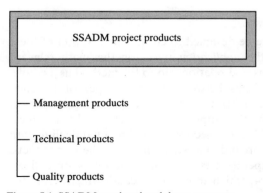

Figure 5.1 SSADM product breakdown structure.

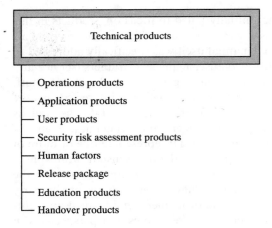

Figure 5.2 SSADM technical products.

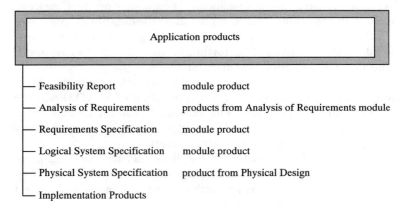

Figure 5.3 SSADM application products.

The standard would therefore be designed to cover only a subset of these products, those identified as the *application type*, together with relevant information on their interactions and relationship to the method as a whole. The SSADM manual distinguishes between different types of product, following on the precepts of PRINCE—the UK government project management framework. Only the application subset of the technical products was specifically SSADM. The sections of the manual dealing with these products also offered breakdown structures of these products, illustrating the component dependencies of groups of items or deliverables—see, for example, Fig. 5.4, which shows the breakdown structure for the Processing Specification.

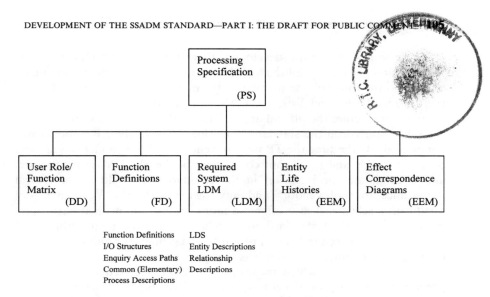

Figure 5.4 SSADM product breakdown structure of processing specification product(s).

The result of these deliberations was a title for the standard: A Standard for the Specification for IS Development Products Using SSADM. This seemed to resolve the matter, but unfortunately it proved not to be the case. Part of the problem may have derived from some of these decisions being taken before the TP had actually seen a near-complete and final draft of Version 4 itself. In addition, the title might have seemed to evolve from the early statement of purpose which proposed a standard 'to enable specification of IS development products in procurement'; but the same document then subverted or dissipated that focus by adding 'to provide a basis for software tools and training' (revised proposal circulated at the meeting 14 June 1990). The later development of the standard provides an object lesson in the consequences of failing to resolve, unambiguously, conceptual issues such as scope and purpose at the outset.

THE ERA MODEL

An additional complication at this early stage was the role of the ERA model of the method. An informal model for Version 3 had been developed sometime after the appearance of Version 3 itself. It consisted of a diagram relating the products of SSADM to each other. It could be drawn on a single sheet of A2, and served as a very useful navigation aid to the method. There were some points on which it was criticized, such as its use of an entity modelling notation different from that used by SSADM itself, but in general it represented a useful overview for Version 3.

As Version 4 was being developed, there was a feeling that a similar exercise should be accomplished, and should form an officially sanctioned adjunct to the four-volume manual of the method itself. This would prove useful to methods specialists, and CASE tool suppliers in particular.

Some time before the official appearance of the manual, and thus before work had started on the standard, the appearance of the ERA model was announced. By the time the TP was convened, the ERA model was spoken of as a tangible and significant component of the SSADM infrastructure, and a candidate for inclusion in the standard. It would be of critical importance to tool vendors and any successor to the Version 3 tool certification scheme. It also offered a more definite and explicit basis upon which to establish a standard for products, since the relationships and dependencies between individual products and groups of products would be clarified and affirmed—or so it was thought.

At the meeting at which members of the TP received the immediate prepublication copy of Version 4, a draft form of the ERA model was circulated. This was far larger and more complex than its Version 3 predecessor. It included a data dictionary—entity definitions and attribute descriptions—amounting to more than 400 pages, with a further 20 or so sheets of large, complex diagrams. This was not an overview model of the method, but a very detailed technical specification—providing it was accurate. It appeared to offer very useful information for the tool vendors, who could treat it as an initial specification for their SSADM CASE offerings, but its usefulness to others was difficult to ascertain.

Two features of the ERA model were critical:

1. Its extension well beyond recognized SSADM application products to include such diverse aspects as team members and roles, modelling concepts, physical report formats and items, and products not mentioned in the manuals.
2. Its organization was not in terms of stages or modules.

This made it difficult to reconcile with a product-based standard. Including it as part of such a document would lead to difficulties in aligning it with the rest of the standard, particularly since the structural model is stage/module based.

Anyone looking over the recorded minutes of TP meetings from that date on (August 1990) will note the appearance of an item on the ERA model for many meetings thereafter, consistently urging a response regarding its role in the standard, and calls for its distribution to a wider audience. At the launch of the Draft for Public Comment (DPC) in June 1991, the matter remained unresolved, although representatives from both the CCTA and the BSI announced a plan to make copies available to interested parties once the five volumes of the DPC were completed. The only problem alluded to was the physical one of photocopying the large sheets on which the model was printed. For reasons other than this, the offer of wider circulation was finally withdrawn later in the year. (The idea of a model of SSADM, a meta-model, seems to have a life of its own. Recent moves to update SSADM make mention of such a meta-model, but unfortunately the lessons of the Version 4 model, and other meta-models of methods, do not seem to have been taken to heart. It seems clear to me that using even an extended ERA notation for this type of model is inadequate, and fails to encompass the purpose and use of such technical matters. There is a very strong, and largely unchallenged argument that more precise and mathematically rigorous notations are demanded for this sort of exercise. That such approaches can and do work is evidenced by work done to integrate structured and formal methods [see for instance Aujla, *et al.*, 1994].)

REPRESENTING AND CLASSIFYING VIEWPOINTS

At these early meetings of the TP, apart from discussions on the scope and title of the standard, those in attendance were keen to know more about standards in general. Agenda items included compliance of the standard with BS0, and a request for a mock-up of the SSADM standard from the CCTA, since many were interested to see what such a document might look like. Fortunately the work of the panel was supported by a considerable input of resources from the CCTA. They supplied the convenor and secretary, both closely involved in the development of Version 4, and each able to devote additional time to the tasks required to progress the early work on the standard. This enabled a good deal of progress to be made, and also supplied a central control on the work of the panel.

In these early stages there was also a considerable amount of input from the voluntary members. One important aspect of this was the extended discussions which sought to satisfy the disparate interests represented. This was eventually documented in the form of a set of distinct viewpoints, each of which had a range of concerns and responsibilities, and hence a particular relationship to the method (SSADM), and by implication to the standard. There were several variants of this, but the overall range of viewpoints proposed (July 1990) was as follows:

1. *Procurer* The procurers' interests include an awareness of the overall structure of the project in order to monitor progress. This requires an overview of the main stages and activities of the method, as well as a concern with the products associated with each stage and/or module. The standard should therefore enable procurement for individual stages or modules: a new contractor could then be expected to tender for a project

in which the products of earlier stages were used as 'raw materials' for later ones.

2. *Tool vendor*   The tool vendor would require the most detailed form of standard, or rather the most precise specification of the entire method. This would have to incorporate the overall structure of the method in terms of sequences of activities, stages, and so on—including inputs and outputs. It would also have to detail the relationships between products—dependencies and correlations. In short, it demanded the ERA model, or something functionally equivalent, or better. In addition, some aspect of the techniques of SSADM, and the semantic and syntactic rules of notations used in the models, would also need to be a component.

3. *Quality assurance*   The QA role would require a standard of appropriate form and application, consistent with general quality standards such as the ISO9000 series. The stages and steps of SSADM would need to be clearly defined, as would the relevant inputs and outputs. Criteria for validation and verification (V&V) would have to be mentioned, together with completion criteria for each step and stage. The QA role also required acceptance criteria for documentation of requirements. If the development path for each product needed to be traced, then something along the lines of the ERA model would need to be a component. At this point panel members realized that there was a problem relating to the extent and detail necessary for inclusion of these criteria in the standard itself. Perhaps other standards, such as ISO9000, provide the detail and a framework for these concerns; or was a detailed SSADM-specific QA sequence required—and should it be part of a single standard?

4. *Trainer*   The trainer's main interest was in the details of the development process itself, in order that any training offered would ensure that trainees could quickly become effective in using SSADM. Thus the material relating to the method must be very detailed, particularly with regard to the overall structure, the range of products, the priority of requirements, details of the techniques, the syntax and semantics of the notations.

5. *Trainee and training accreditors*   Same as trainers.

6. *Designers and consultants*   Here the main concern was the satisfaction of procurement/client requirements through use of SSADM. This would probably require less detailed specification of the details of the method, particularly the techniques, than for the trainers, since fulfilment of client SSADM requirements may be possible and even desirable without applying the method in detail.

7. *Users*   This referred to users of SSADM, not users of the information system itself. These practitioners would make day-to-day use of the reference manual plus other support material.

8. *Suppliers of reference material, guides, and the like*   These could use the standard as the definition of mandatory features of SSADM (a

misunderstanding of the role of both SSADM and of standards). In order for this to be accomplished the relationship between these materials (including the reference manuals) and the standard would have to clarified (a prescient point here—see below).

These eight viewpoints were tabled as part of the general consideration of the SSADM domain. It was never intended that all aspects of all viewpoints could or should be covered by the standard. The QA aspect, in particular, demonstrated that many of the issues went far beyond the confines of the method, and encroached upon aspects in which standards already existed, and to which the SSADM standard probably ought to refer. The result was that the eight viewpoints were refined into a smaller number of 'interfaces', and since BS0 specifically mentioned interfaces, this emphasized the role of a standard as facilitating exchange and transactions.

BSI policy is to supply standards that will address the supplier/customer interface. The TP interpreted this as requiring a clear statement in the introduction to the standard, defining all relevant interfaces addressed by the standard. Unfortunately custom and practice in the BSI dictates that a single standard should be oriented around a single interface (this is not actually documented in BS0, but was made clear at later editorial stages). This makes sense, since otherwise a standard will lack a clear and straightforward audience. Unfortunately this was not realized at this early stage, and the DPC made mention of eight interfaces in all five volumes.

With hindsight it is ironic that the minutes from one of the earliest meetings of the panel (August 1990) include the observation that BS0 defines a specification-type standard as the basis for understanding between a purchaser and a supplier. In noting this in the minutes, the point is immediately restated, contradicted, and finally dissipated.

> The standard will therefore be expressed in terms of two viewpoints only, Purchaser/Supplier, and will limit itself to addressing the definition of IS development products in terms relevant to suppliers of services in the IS development area, appropriate tools and training.

(NB: This is as much an admonition of the members of the TP, as it is indicative of the problems of seeking to achieve a complex aim without the benefit of expert guidance from those with relevant experience.)

THE SCOPE AND LEVEL OF DETAIL

One crucial agenda item for the initial meetings of the TP was to resolve the level of detail at which the standard should be pitched. SSADM is divided into levels with modules consisting of one or two stages, each of which has numerous steps. In particular, discussion centred on the details relating to the activities of the method, i.e. the procedures rather than the products. One contribution noted five possible levels of detail, ranging from 0 up to 4:

4 full details of all steps
3 outline details of all steps
2 inclusion of all steps by name, plus brief outline of procedure
1 inclusion of all steps by name
0 steps omitted.

The idea was that a rating for each of the eight viewpoints should be selected—although it was argued that the QA aspect was identical to that of procurement. On the other hand, this same proposal suggested that rather than seeing each viewpoint as an isolated perspective, a matrix of all possible relationships between viewpoints should be considered, and attention then focused on the key intersections in the matrix. This argument highlighted an important aspect of any contractual context for the development of IS products or services, but it was not suited to the purpose in hand, being too complex and sophisticated to guide the deliberations of the panel. In essence it moved too far from the stated, but increasingly neglected, objective of a product-oriented standard.

At around this time (August 1990) the final and complete draft of the Version 4 manuals was distributed to members of the TP. This amounted to four very large volumes detailing the method. As has already been stated, Version 4 sought to stress that the method was not meant to be treated as a strict procedure, but as the basis for a flexible framework. Progress through the method was charted by delivery of products.

The sheer volume of material in the manuals, plus the unresolved aspects of the deliberations of the panel, inhibited the work of the panel. Those attending the meetings just could not maintain sufficient impetus outside the meetings to deal with the many actions and tasks required to progress the standard. More critically, they could not justify expenditure of extra resources on this project to their sponsoring organizations.

Fortunately the CCTA had decided to allocate resources to the development of the standard. They had their own set of objectives to be met. This might have meant that the standard would not be arrived at by consensus, but by assent to whatever the CCTA produced, or simply by default. In fact this did not happen because a series of mechanisms were employed both by the CCTA and the BSI to ensure that a true consensus could emerge. In some respects it might be argued that some of these mechanisms should have been deployed earlier in the process, but it is doubtful if this would have avoided some of the revisions and re-evaluations that distinguished the development of the standard. In any case, it would be entirely unjustified to remark that because the CCTA supplied all the major resources, the standard bore the imprint of the CCTA's concept of what the standard ought to be. In fact the final outcome bore little resemblance to anyone's initial suppositions.

At least with a title, and a full draft of the reference manual, some of the panel's decisions could be taken with an eye to the actual content of the standard. With the text of the manual available electronically, the temptation might have been simply to 'reconstruct' the manual superficially and place BSI covers around the eventual document. This might at least have met the objective of accommodating the method in the EC single market, but it would not have met the objective of a usable, product-oriented standard. Further meetings of the TP, however, failed to retain this objective at the forefront of their work, and gradually additional layers of complications and details obscured what had promised to be a manageable scope.

By late 1990 a number of issues on the scope and nature of the standard were emerging as dominant themes—though not all of these were central to the standardization of SSADM itself. These latter ones in particular diluted the focus of attention of a product-based SSADM standard. For instance the panel spent time considering issues such as the links between the SSADM standard and emerging repository standards such as IRDS, (Information Resource Dictionary Standard), as well as the general issue regarding exchange of machine-readable information concerning SSADM projects. This then extended the discussion into the form the standard should take: whether it should be fundamentally textual (including diagrams), or in parts more formally defined (see below). Other decisions specifically precluded extraneous issues: it had been agreed that the process of devising the standard for SSADM (and the developing work on the real-time approach MASCOT) should not be taken as an exemplar of the necessary path for the standardization of any other method, i.e. the panel was not seeking to develop a standard for producing methods standards.

The objective of specifying a product-based standard was further complicated by differing views of the prerequisites for defining SSADM standards; and for whom they were to be defined. Again, had the most rudimentary interpretation of the customer/supplier interface been adhered to, many of the ensuing issues might not have arisen, and to an extent this view was upheld in the conclusion that at least all non-human interfaces were to be excluded from consideration, at least at this early stage. This meant that the machine-readable and information-exchange aspects could be dispensed with, as the standard would be constrained by interhuman interfaces.

This brought two main issues to the forefront:

- What was the minimum set of product descriptions (taken from Volume 4 of the reference manual) to be included in the standard?

- What additional material needed to be included as the packaging and support for these products specifications?

One interpretation held that since the products embodied and relied upon the SSADM modelling concepts, the prerequisite for specifying the products was a definition of the concepts. These were defined adequately in the reference manual, in various sections of the four volumes. Each product could therefore include a reference to the relevant section(s) of the manual.

Unfortunately this possibility was deemed unsuitable since the TP had been advised (incorrectly as it transpired) that standards should not refer to external documents apart from other standards. Given this constraint, there would have to be at least two standards: one for modelling concepts, and one for products. In addition, if the standard was to appear as several volumes, each volume had to be self-contained, and care had to be taken to avoid circular references (e.g. in Volume 1, Section B.3 might make reference to Volume 2, Section C.1; and Volume 2, C.1 might make reference to Volume 1, B.3—with neither clarifying the exact details involved).

These two points taken together meant that the volumes would have to duplicate material already contained in the reference manual, and would even have to duplicate material across separate volumes of the standard.

A careful study of BS0 would have quickly shown the TP that these opinions concerning referencing other publications and sources were incorrect. Although the BSI takes great care to furnish copies of the most recent edition of BS0 to panel participants, and even lodges further copies in many of its committee rooms, panel members failed to refer to BS0 at this stage. Had this been done, perhaps some of the problems with the DPC would not have arisen.

The introduction of modelling concepts as part of the standard led to consideration of the best way of representing these concepts. In the manuals they are explained in textual terms, with some diagrammatic illustrations. For most purposes, and most audiences, this is perfectly adequate.

But since the issues of data exchange and information repositories had been introduced, the possibility of a more rigorous or formal representation was discussed. This introduced mention of topics such as IRDS and even formal (mathematically based) notations such as VDM and Z.

It was at this time that some members of the panel became concerned that they were losing sight of the scope of the standard, and moving well beyond any realistic constraints. A letter to the panel from one of its members voiced these concerns as follows:

> In response to the meeting of the BSI panel on SSADM last week, I enclose a few comments which I trust you will be able to incorporate into a paper for general discussion at the next meeting.
>
> 1. I think it must constantly be borne in mind that the title for the standard stresses 'Specification for IS *Products* using SSADM'. At the time that this was

resolved there were extensive discussions concerning whether or not the standard would be process or product oriented. The latter was seen as preferable. The standard could then serve as an interface between parties at different, specified stages of development. While bearing in mind that the 'deliverables' must be couched in terms of the method (SSADM), to some extent these must be conceptual and generic rather than too closely identified with specific SSADM forms or tangible products.

2. The major question then becomes one of analyzing the current state of the SSADM documentation of 'products' and amending them to some acceptable range of uniformity, or limited set of categories. The product descriptions currently vary from reference to a document or report, to something more substantive involving a syntax or semantic model, implying a technique or range of techniques. I do not think it feasible or even possible that these could all be restructured into a single common format, and so I suggest a limited set of categories. At this stage I am not in a position to suggest candidate types!

3. The aim of some IRDS meta-model of SSADM is really too far off to be a realistic target or guiding objective at this stage. There may well be possible ways of modelling the products, but I am not sure whether there is a role for object-oriented or even formal models in a published SSADM standard in the present climate.

4. The introduction of a focus on the modelling concepts may help in classifying the products. I do not see that it would be necessary to go much further than data, process, event.

5. The essential contents of the standard must include a refined set of product descriptions, possibly differentiating between mandatory, alternative, and desirable deliverables. These must in some way be linked to stages of the SSADM cycle. Clearly any one product will have a life cycle within the development cycle. One possible way forward would be for a 'complete' list of all SSADM product descriptions to be drawn up. These could then be treated to an ELH type of analysis, where the event nodes are stages/modules. A set of ECDs could then be generated to link all these ELHs. I realize that this is a complex project, but I do not think that the ERA model on its own will be sufficient.

6. With reference to the RS module—this consists of 1 stage, 8 steps, plus a list of preconditions, and management authorizations. 4 Products are listed, but it would be more accurate to term these 4 categories of product, since some of them—e.g. Requirements Specification—clearly imply a set of related products evolving over the development span. Similarly the list of techniques is not comprehensive, since some techniques are possibly implied by lower level products. In the light of what I have suggested above, it would appear to be best to restrict the standard to the 'step' level. Products will then need to be defined at the necessary level of detail. Looking through the Dictionary, much of the information is already there, even if the form and weighting of the contents might need alteration. There are, however, several weak areas—e.g. 'Installation Style Guide', which appears as a precondition to the stage, but is not really described at any level of useful detail.

7. Some aspects of the dictionary need close attention—e.g. the method of 'formal review' is mentioned in several entries, but does not appear as an entry in itself.

These points and other similar concerns were not heeded, however, and the idea of several related standards took root. This involved a repackaging, although not a reworking, of a large proportion of the reference manual. It also increasingly sought to facilitate extensions into the realm of IRDS and the ISO domain in general.

THE FIVE-VOLUME DPC

By late 1990, or early 1991, a shape for the set of SSADM standards had begun to emerge. The overall standard would encompass concepts, products, and notations, as well as modules and stages. Much of the material from the manuals would be incorporated, but in a slightly different arrangement. In format the full SSADM standard would actually consist of four main standards, plus an additional standard defining how the four parts related to one another. The five volumes would include a framework standard, a product standard, a concepts standard, a steps and stages standard, and a presentation standard.

The *framework* standard would define the overall scope and structure of the five volumes, and the relationship to the method. It would also include a list of all definitions and abbreviations.

The *modelling concepts* standard would explain the key concepts grouped into the domains of activity given in the manuals. This listed 13 concepts, such as entity-event modelling, data flow modelling, and so on.

The *presentation conventions* standard would define the representational rules associated with the relevant modelling concepts.

The *basic product descriptions* standard would paraphrase relevant entries from the manual. The products would be grouped into the 13 categories used in the modelling concepts standard, with two additional categories. Each entry would have details for its description and purpose, composition, derivation, and quality criteria.

The *modules and stages* standard would cover the major activities, showing the objectives, participants, and preconditions for each, as well as the products and techniques. Detailed descriptions of the steps would be omitted.

This appeared attractive at first sight since any one of the four component standards could be altered to some extent without impacting on the others. For instance, if the presentation conventions changed, there might be no reason to change the conceptual bases. The downside was that the five volumes were at least as large as the reference manuals, duplicated material from those manuals and across the volumes themselves, and lacked a clear scope and target audience or interface.

Without realizing it, the TP had lost direction and focus; or rather they had attempted to encompass too many disparate centres of attention, e.g. trainers, CASE tool vendors, QA people, and so on, as well as customers and suppliers. The original eight viewpoints had been reduced, but this had been done by amalgamating aspects rather than by concentrating on specific ones. In addition a further interface, to IRDS, had been added.

In attempting to embrace this disparate range of interests, and by adding all the concomitant details, the panel had also dissipated the originally agreed idea of a standard for IS *products* using SSADM. One reason for this loss or lack of direction was that from the start it appeared that the standardization effort for SSADM was likely to have repercussions well beyond the confines of UK and the method itself; even at the first meeting of the panel the topic of 'European and international developments' was aired. This simply added to the complications and exposed the lack of experience of the panel, and so served to diffuse the overall focus of the members.

Even before some of these problems became apparent there were other difficulties. The volume on presentation conventions was proving particularly problematic. The concern was not to allow it to be too restrictive and normative. The reference manuals offered examples of representations for models such as data flow diagrams, data models, and so on. The particular representations used were drawn from the range of those available and recognized by practitioners across the world. They therefore embodied a clear preference, excluding some notations, appearing to favour others. On the other hand, the manuals were at pains to point out that SSADM was not meant to mandate a specific set of conventions. The diagrams in the manuals were only included for illustration. This had been mentioned specifically in order that developers, CASE suppliers, trainers, and so on would feel less constrained in using the method. The inclusion of any notation in the standard would, however, seem to favour (if not almost mandate) a particular convention.

One solution appeared to be to include several options in the presentation conventions volume. For instance, there seemed to be two main forms of indicating sub/super-type hierarchies on entity models. These could both be exemplified in the relevant sections of the standard. The only problem would then be that other options would have been excluded.

Another issue arose with regard to the 'official' SSADM forms included in the manuals, and by this time available commercially from NCC. These forms could potentially contain a great deal of information relevant to the development project. This might include conceptual assumptions, priorities, constraints, and so on. Where would this sort of information be covered in the standard? Would it make sense to include the forms as part of the standard? (In the manual the forms are attached to the product descriptions, e.g. the form for External Entity Descriptions is exemplified in the entry in Volume 4 for that product. [There is also an entry for the 'Generic Blank Form'.] To the newly initiated SSADM practitioners the forms are a key product; to the more experienced they are simply a minor embodiment of SSADM concepts. This tension between the novice and the expert remains unresolved as discussion develops about the directions for SSADM post-1994.)

It was strongly argued that in a fashion similar to that for the presentation conventions, the forms were meant to be illustrative rather than definitive: including specific forms, explicitly depicted, in the standard would undermine this view. Furthermore there was an unresolved question relating to the ownership and copyright of the forms. One opinion held that the forms were in the public domain, the other that they were the copyright either of the HMSO (Crown copyright) or NCC/Blackwell (publishers of the manuals).

A further issue arose from the realization that many organizations did not use the complete SSADM, and adapted parts of it as required. Should the standard include a suggested or recommended procedure for tailoring the method? If so, what would such a procedure need to detail? Would this entail defining mandatory and optional parts of SSADM—directly contradicting the reference manual statement on the philosophy of the method—and should those mandatory and optional parts be products, processes, or techniques? Indeed should the standard refer to sequences of stages at all, since again this would imply a prescribed route through the method? (Again this sort of argument pre-empts the current arguments about 'flexible' SSADM. The DAB are caught in the tension between the growing body of experienced SSADM practitioners and the continuing need to train novice users. Attempts to move beyond Version 4 by relaxing the constraints of the method need to find a generally acceptable statement of the 'essence of SSADM', i.e. what remains after the *optional* aspects have been isolated. To date this has not been done, although the standard does offer a possible basis for a solution.)

Generally these three issues emanated from a misconception regarding standards; standards are not necessarily mandatory, or rather not all aspects of standards are obligatory. On the other hand, since this misconception is widespread in the community at large, it was important that the flexibility of SSADM was not undermined by seemingly constraining aspects of the method.

Another main item discussed at TP meetings at this stage concerned the way in which any inconsistencies in the reference manuals should be treated. Since the manuals were extensive, and newly released, a certain number of errors were bound to be discovered. Some of these might be quite trivial; others more profound or extensive. Should the standard correct these defects, or reproduce them and remain aligned with the manuals? After all, with the dubious exception of the ERA model, the standard was meant to be an accurate subset of the reference manuals. The matter was not resolved at the time of the publication of the DPC, but the CCTA hinted at the appearance of a revision or errata list sometime after the publication of the manuals in 1990–91.

Eventually the five-volume DPC appeared in June 1991. In normal circumstances the appearance of a DPC is announced in the BSI publication *BSI News*. The relevant technical committees are also informed, and copies—or extracts—supplied to members. For the SSADM standard the TP were fortunate to have the backing of the SSADM Users Group. They agreed to host the launch of the DPC, arranging a central venue, and purchasing bulk copies of the DPC so that all those attending would be supplied with the documents. The launch was attended by more than 100 people, and they were all able to take four of the five volumes with them; the fifth (presentation conventions) was not then available, but was dispatched to all participants a few weeks later.

The presentations by members of the TP, and the BSI (DISC) covered the reasons for developing a standard for SSADM, the structure of the five volumes, and the details of the components. The mood of the audience was generally supportive, although some were a little perplexed, asking 'why was a standard needed?'; 'who would use it?'; 'how would they use it?'; 'what effect would it have on procurement, on suppliers, and on other methods?' These were all dealt with in the ensuing discussions, as was the predictable request for the ERA model. The members of the TP went away relatively satisfied with the response, having stressed that the documents be studied carefully, and that those with comments should ensure that they were sent to the BSI by the deadline in three months' time.

6

THE DEVELOPMENT OF THE SSADM STANDARD—PART II: RESPONDING TO THE DPC, AND EVENTUAL PUBLICATION

RESPONSES TO THE DPC

Although the TP had never attempted to conceal its work, and certain members had even gone to great lengths to disclose its progress to wider audiences, it was only with the launch of the DPC that the matter received any sort of prominence even among SSADM practitioners.

Computing covered the matter in two short articles in June and July 1991. (The later one reported the official launch of the DPC—see Chapter 5.) The earlier one was headlined 'CCTA surrender casts a shadow over SSADM' (20 June). The article reported that SSADM users were worried that the BSI rather than the CCTA were going to become controllers of the method, and that 'any modifications to the core method ... would have to be authorised by a BSI committee'. Representatives from the Users Group, the National Computing Centre, and the CCTA were quoted. All agreed that the appearance of a standard for SSADM would constrain the development of the method, but all of them saw positive benefits from a standard. The *Computing* article did voice genuine concerns, and these were repeated, with some feeling, at the SSADM Users Group meeting in September.

The SSADM UG holds two main gatherings each year. The spring meeting is usually held for one day and takes place in London; the autumn conference is residential and lasts two or three days. In September 1991, the meeting was held in Cambridge, and began with a technical day including tutorial sessions on some of the new Version 4 techniques and notations, and a special session on the standard.

The UG had commissioned a formal presentation responding to the DPC, and this was to be followed by an open session from the audience. Some of those attending had been at the launch of the DPC; some had had sight of the DPC itself; most were merely aware that the standard was progressing. The session started with a brief overview of the five volumes of the DPC. The formal presentation then took the form of a set of fairly detailed responses from two members of the UG representing a user (BT) and a methods supplier (LBMS).

The main points raised were as follows:

1. There was too much detail in the standard, making it cumbersome and inflexible—contrary to the SSADM philosophy.
2. The language was poor or opaque, and there were many places where punctuation and grammar needed correction.
3. The main terms were defined in each volume; this was unnecessary and would create problems if certain items were later revised.
4. Some definitions were circular, and some were incorrect—there was particular concern at the definition of 'event' which differed from that in the manual.
5. Some errors in the manuals had been incorporated without comment or revision in the DPC.

The conclusion was that the DPC formed a basis for standardization, but should not be seen as approximating to the finished standard itself.

The concerns expressed by members of the audience echoed some of these points, but added many more. Opinion was divided on whether the standard would prove harmful or beneficial. Those speaking from the procurement side of the customer/supplier interface seemed enthusiastic. The standard would help them in negotiations with suppliers, and would prevent lock-in to particular sources of services or products. Those on the supplier side were less convinced, and in effect argued that perhaps many involved in procurement did not understand the full complexity of systems development and delivery, and would see the standard as an easy way out. The temptation would be to demand strict adherence to the standard, rather than to see the standard as a basis for negotiation. (A similar point had been made at the launch of the DPC.)

Not surprisingly many of the issues discussed by the TP surfaced at the UG meeting; however, the conclusions were not always the same. Some advocated that the BSI should first establish a general standard for methods, and only then seek to standardize a specific method. Others said that despite assurances from the TP, the SSADM standard would be considered as a paradigm for other methods standards, and so it was important that it was seen to have been done properly and correctly.

There was general concern at the level of detail in the DPC, and the repetition involved across the five volumes. The minimalist view was that the standard should really be a simple statement of purpose about the need for a public and quotable SSADM standard, followed by a reference to the current version of the manual. This should be sufficient to satisfy the EC regulations. The maximalist view, on the other hand, was that the standard should cover the entire material of the manual, including full descriptions of steps and stages, and techniques. In effect, the reference manuals with BSI covers.

The argument centring on what aspect of SSADM was being standardized was also touched upon. Many were keen that the procedures of SSADM should be standardized—by which they really meant enforced. It was, however, stressed that this was not achievable through a standard, even if it was desirable. There were others who thought a product-based standard was desirable and sufficient.

Several comments arose requesting clarification of the relationship between the BSI and the DAB. Reports such as those in the *Computing* article suggested that the latter would be very clearly subordinate to the former. This might be acceptable, providing that the constitution and membership of the BSI panel reflected the interests of the SSADM community, rather than simply the standards community. On the other hand, if the standard was controlled by the BSI and the method by the DAB, what mechanisms would be established to deal with change control and integrity between the two? Could the situation arise in which the standard referred to one variant of the method, and the reference manual to another? This line of thought extended to querying the relationship to programmes such as the ISEB training and the Tool Conformance schemes.

More specific comments focused on how different presentation conventions could be accommodated in the standard. This sort of comment partly arise from the mistaken belief that a standard was a statement of obligation, and hence mandated specific aspects. On the other hand, if one type of representation was given in the standard, even merely as one among several possibilities, it would almost certainly gain over its alternatives.

Others wanted to know about the status of the ERA model. Was it to be part of the standard, and if so how would it align with the five volumes of the DPC? Those with experience of quality standards such as BS5750 (ISO 9000) wanted to know how the SSADM standard would relate to these other ones.

These latter points were relatively easy to clarify. The earlier ones had to a large extent been ignored by the TP, and would need to brought into consideration with some urgency—and certainly resolved before any further progress towards a standard could be made.

A number of other issues arose, mostly from those seeking advice on how to use a standard. It was asked why there was no guidance in the DPC concerning how the standard should be used; how conformance to the standard should be judged, especially for the volume concerned with the modelling concepts; how the standard should function as a baseline for defining the method; how the standard should be policed; and how the standard would operate in the wider EC context.

At the most fundamental level, the need for a standard for SSADM was questioned. Using (Version 3) SSADM terminology, it was asked: 'What is the entry on the Problem Requirements List for which the SSADM standard is the solution?' Added to which members of the UG expressed the fear that the standard would fossilize and solidify SSADM practices: As one earlier correspondent put it:

> If the standard becomes too rigid, defining the methodology too precisely and with little leeway, it will become a contractual nightmare. Whilst even a user company may agree that one aspect of the methodology is not significant for their own particular project, they will feel contractually bound to require it. (Tony Marshall, then Chair of SSADM UG Future Development Subgroup, April 1990)

The overall response of the UG, by this time representing over 400 organizations, was profound scepticism and in some cases hostility. The meeting closed with a request from the UG Technical Committee for as many as possible to submit responses concerning the DPC to the BSI, and also to the UG itself, which would be preparing a formal response.

THE CHANGING EC CONTEXT

One of the simple answers to the question concerning the need for the standard was that it appeared to be a way of satisfying EC regulations, while permitting continued mention of SSADM in public procurement exercises, and as part of ITTs. By the middle of 1991, however, this was no longer the case. A judgement by the European Court (C45/87) had caused the EC Supplies Directive to be clarified with regard to national standards. Any reference to national standards could not be mandated unless '*equivalent standards* from other member states are also admissible' (italics added).

Although this ruling had not arisen from a dispute concerning IS procurement, it had a clear bearing on SSADM. There were no other member states with any plans for standardizing an IS development method. Indeed there were no other member states with an equivalent to SSADM. The French favoured MERISE, but this was not controlled in one place in the manner that the DAB controlled SSADM. In fact there were several variations of MERISE in use by this time. The Italians had a method called DAFNE, the Dutch SDM, the Spanish MEIN (but they also used SSADM), and the Germans used a variety of methods. No other EC member state had plans to promote a national standard. A requirement in an ITT for SSADM, or 'its equivalent', would not be permitted even if incorporated in the form of a reference to a British Standard.

The details of this EC decision, and a restatement of the CCTA position regarding the standard, were contained in IS Notice 26, issued within UK government circles in July 1991. Unfortunately the document was not circulated more widely until well after the UG meeting in September.

The IS Notice stressed that the purpose of the standard was that it serve as a 'specification to be used as "a basis for understanding" between a purchaser and a supplier of a SSADM-based service' (IS Notice 26, July 1991, Section 3). The benefits of such a basis for understanding would be that the 'amount of precise specification effort will be greatly reduced, although the accuracy of the defined requirements will be increased' (Section 4). Also the criteria for acceptance and compliance with customer requirements would be easier to state and verify.

The notice included a section on the *supply of systems*. While noting that the standard would not be able to be included in this regard, as a result of the ruling from the European Court, it was pointed out that there was no equivalent directive relating to a requirement for *services*, but this would almost certainly be rectified in due course. The mandating of the standard in any form of procurement was therefore not recommended.

This would not, however, preclude use of the standard, since its application and relevance could form the basis of a discussion between supplier and purchaser. Purchasers were therefore recommended to 'make reference to the standard' (Section 8) in the following fashion.

> The department intends to discuss with suppliers the applicability of BS*nnnn* part *x* to the products and deliverables and BS*nnnn* part *y* to the completion of the activity under mandatory requirements *ppp–qqq*, with a view to incorporating conformance to these standards in any eventual contract.
> Suppliers will not be excluded from consideration if they cannot conform to these standards, but any additional costs that the department consider will arise to it as a result of this non-conformance may be added to a supplier's final tender as an evaluation issue.   (Section 8)

The issue of compatibility with the method was also addressed. The BSI TP would be responsible for ensuring that the standard reflected any changes to the method. There was no specific mention of what would happen if the BSI decided to change the standard for any other reason, which might necessitate a change to the method.

The meetings of the TP planned for September and October had originally been seen as the point at which detailed consideration could be given to the responses received with regard to the DPC. Instead the main items on the agenda reflected the ways in which the entire context of SSADM standardization had altered. The clearest reason for developing the standard had been rendered obsolete, or at least severely curtailed. In addition the DPC itself had been severely criticized at the most fundamental levels. The TP's consideration of the overall mechanisms relating to the standard and the method had been found wanting. To add to this situation of uncertainty, the original convenor and secretary had resigned as both had been reassigned different responsibilities within the CCTA.

The distinction between method and standard remained unresolved. IS Notice 26 had not tackled the full issue, assuming only that the standard would change in response to the method, and not vice versa. This view was echoed by the DAB (see below). One suggestion emanating from the TP was that the panel merge with the DAB, or that the TP take on responsibility for the method as well as the standard. The September meeting of the TP decided to invite the entire DAB to the next panel meeting to discuss this; but the DAB rejected this in favour of more limited and formal liaison. (The TP convenor would be invited to join DAB, attending meetings in that capacity.)

To add to this state of disorientation, issues regarding the copyright of the material from the SSADM manuals had arisen. It had previously been assumed that this would not be a problem since the manuals were under the control of the CCTA. It now transpired that although the manuals were published by a private company (NCC/Blackwell), they remained Crown copyright, and this could not be reassigned. On the other hand, BSI policy was that anything published by the BSI was their copyright.

RECONSTITUTING THE TECHNICAL PANEL—RECASTING THE STANDARD

In October 1991 the TP reconvened in an expanded form. Since the original representative of the UG (and author of this book) had now become convenor, and as a result of the high profile given to the standard at the UG autumn meeting, a number of additional UG members were now involved in the work of the panel. One represented the Technical Committee, others were there in other capacities, such as ISEB or TCS, and some simply as individuals. This changed the overall balance of the panel, in that most of those attending had considerable expertise in SSADM, and a profound stake in the development of SSADM products and services.

The paramount concern of the meeting was to examine the continuing requirement for a standard in the light of the EC ruling. The panel considered aborting the process, but eventually decided to continue with the development of the standard. Although the EC position was now somewhat equivocal, the work on the standard had achieved a certain level of recognition and so it was important that it not simply cease. The EC position was that a single national standard may not be used in isolation, since it effectively bars all other options. The committee therefore had to consider the likely future developments. If the SSADM standard was liable to be the first of several forays into the standards-for-methods arena, then the anomaly of being the sole such standard might be short-lived. In this case it would be important that some form of positive precedent was set: the SSADM standard must be seen to have been successful, the process of arriving at its final form must be reasonably well accepted, and the main issues of standardizing a method must have been considered and resolved.

If, more likely, other EC members were unlikely to follow this course, then the pioneering aspect of the standard in this sense ceased to be relevant. The panel then needed to consider the role and purpose of a standard for SSADM. It might be that the standard was of relevance in a less direct sense, but this alone could not justify its existence.

The announcement from the CCTA clarifying the position following the EC ruling (IS Notice 26, July 1991) had stressed the continuing need for a standard. Essentially this could be stated as follows:

> The purpose of the standard is to provide a basis for agreement between customer and a service provider about the work to be undertaken using SSADM.
>
> One benefit of the standard would be to reduce greatly the 'precise specification effort', but increase the accuracy in defining exact requirements.
>
> Another benefit would be more straightforward agreement on the 'criteria against which compliance with the customer's requirements can subsequently be verified'. (IS Notice 26, Section 3)

The panel was broadly in agreement with this statement, although there was some consternation that it had not been available to the UG meeting in September: it would have helped clarify many of the points which arose. That apart, there was overwhelming support for a product-based standard, although it would be preferable if the bulk of detail in the DPC could be jettisoned in favour of references to the relevant sections of the manual.

This reintroduced the question of referring to external sources. Taking the opportunity to study the copy of BS0 available in the meeting room, it appeared the panel had allowed themselves to be misdirected regarding the issue of reference to non-BSI sources in the standard. According to BS0 (1991)—Part 3, Section 3.5.2.1—there are conditions where it is permissible to refer to non-BSI publications as normative, as opposed to informative, sources. (Normative elements of a standard are defined in BS0 as 'those setting out the essential provisions of a standard, i.e. those with which it is necessary to comply in order to be able to claim compliance with the standard' [BS0, Part 3, 3.1]. Informative elements are those that add background or supplementary features.) Eight criteria are listed under this heading, and after some discussion it was felt that all could be satisfied:

1. *'Publication cited has wide acceptance and authoritative status'* This applied to the current manuals, and presumably would continue to do so

if the CCTA or the DAB could confirm the likely future arrangements for revision and new versions. The ISEB would need to confirm the same if the Certificate of Proficiency (COP) scheme were to be referenced. Similarly for any mention of the Tools Conformance Scheme

2. *'Reference to the publication is unambiguous and dated'* All references would need to state SSADM version number and date. This implied issues of change control, but these could be accomplished by reissue of the standard or a simple notification if necessary.
3. *'The publication does not depend upon further reference to non-BSI publications'* This might have been problematic for the manuals, but in fact the manuals do not *depend* upon other sources, even if they make references to other material. The ISEB documentation, on the other hand, certainly does refer to the manuals.
4. *'Publication is readily available'* The manual is readily available.
5. *'Source from which copies of the publication can be obtained is stated'* Again not a problem since the manuals are officially published and recorded with ISBN details.
6. *'A master copy of the publication is retained for reference in the BSI Library'* Arrangements would be made for representatives of the CCTA, the ISEB, etc., to lodge copies with the BSI.
7. *'Body responsible for the publication is informed of BSI's intention to refer to it and is asked to notify BSI as early as possible of any decision to amend, revise or withdraw it'* The DAB would be asked to confirm this.
8. *'Any relevant government regulatory and enforcement authorities confirm that for their purposes it is sufficient to make the reference'* There was some discussion of what was included in the phrase 'relevant government authorities', but this did not seem problematic.

Since there seemed a strong case in favour of referring to the SSADM manuals in this way, and all the criteria could be met, it was agreed to advise the Deputy Director (BSI) that the panel wished to proceed on the basis of using the reference manuals as normative references, and also to seek confirmation from the CCTA that copyright would not be infringed (BS0, Part 3:15.5).

In terms of dealing with the responses to the DPC, and devising a plan of work to move from DPC to published standard, it was agreed that panel members should try to identify areas in which work might be needed, and estimate the resources required. Panel members were also to be allocated one volume of the DPC for which to produce comments and a revision plan. The UG agreed to assist in more general ways with the quality assurance for the later drafts.

This seemed a sound basis to continue development of the standard, but two issues remained outstanding: the ERA model, and the relationship between the DAB and the BSI.

The DISC had by this time agreed to fund the production of copies of the ERA model. But panel members felt that perhaps the model was not 'fit for purpose', and that its complexity and variances from the manual might mean that its distribution to a wider audience would be counterproductive. On the other hand, any failure to distribute the model might engender suspicion, which would be just as bad. The agreed compromise was to arrange a means of distribution outside the umbrella of the BSI, thus achieving the objective of circulation, but divorcing it from the standard. The UG Technical Committee was therefore asked to investigate the possibility of being the conduit for distributing the model to those members of the UG expressing an interest. The model would have to be published with a 'health warning' stressing that:

1. It is a draft for comment and not an officially sanctioned component of the SSADM standard or manual.
2. Is meant to be a model of products, with reference to the concepts; it is not functionally equivalent to the ERA model for Version 3.

The relationship between the BSI and the DAB, however, remained a stumbling block. The DAB had been formally invited to attend the TP meeting, with a view to merging at a later stage. The DAB had declined this, and affirmed that liaison through the convenor being a member of DAB would be sufficient. The DAB reiterated that in their view they were the guardians of the method, and for that reason held the primary role over the BSI as controllers of the standard. The BSI panel would probably have accepted this, but advice had been sought from the Council of the EC, and it conflicted directly with the DAB's position.

The Chairman of the CEC Public Procurement Group had expressed his own opinion (and not necessarily that of the CEC) on the SSADM standard as follows:

1. It might be legal to include in a statement of Operational Requirements a clause along the lines of: if the supplier intends to use SSADM, then it must comply with the standard.
2. If the standard has been agreed with all parties to the contract, then the standard can be invoked.
3. The standard for SSADM is at a lower level of application than the proposed one for Euromethod. Therefore once (if) the Euromethod framework is in place, the SSADM standard must align with it.
4. There should be a commitment for the standard to migrate as necessary to make it comply with European standards.
5. 'Any statement that the standard will reflect changes to the method implies ownership of the standard by the methods supplier. The standard

must have greater priority and the method (as defined in the manual) must reflect the standard.'

This conflicted explicitly with the position of the DAB. It was not immediately resolved, and to some extent it still remains unresolved at the time of writing (June 1994).

THE RESPONSES TO THE DPC

The most common type of response to the DPC for the SSADM standard focused on the need and desirability for such a standard. This was increasingly pertinent given the change—reversal—in the situation from that which motivated the initial aspirations for the development of a standard. More critically, the potentially negative aspects of the standard needed to be contemplated. The most portentous of these concerned the relationship between the method and the standard. The TP invitation to the DAB was in effect rebuffed, so the position could be reached where a standard was in place, with no explicit relevance to the wider procurement issues, and with no obvious relationship with the method itself. This would be anomalous, inviting discredit on both the standard and the method.

One solution would have been to insist that the standard encompass the method: in effect that control of the two reside with the BSI panel. This would firmly locate SSADM in the public domain. The problem would then arise if deliberations of the panel were to lead to the recommendation of changes to the method. Who would specify these changes? Who would resource development and eventual release of the new version? Where would copyright for the manuals and other support materials reside? What copyright issues would need to be resolved before even the initial release of the standard? Could the standard be abbreviated and refer for detailed technical matters to the 'current version' of the manuals? A summary of the points issues raised in response to the DPC is given in Table 6.1.

Regarding the content of the standard itself, it was now clear that the entire structure of the standard needed examination and revision. From an initial concentration on the products, the standard, in the form of the five-volume DPC, now seemed to have a bearing on all aspects of the development process encompassed by SSADM. This was proving unwieldy.

The ERA model was a particularly contentious issue. There had been attempts to clarify the situation, but the confusion remained. Based on the experience of the Version 3 model, the Version 4 ERA model had been expected by some to resolve issues for tool builders and provide the basis for conformance schemes. Hence the clamour for release of the model as part of the standard. Study of the circulated version of the ERA model did not convince anyone that it would serve this purpose. If the model was to serve as a general overview of the method in terms of products, then it needed to be far less intricate and more compact. If it was to serve as a rigorous basis for tool specification and evaluation, then perhaps an ERA model was not best suited to the purpose.

To summarize, the issues identified at this stage by the newly constituted technical panel were as follows:

1. Current EC position on standards, and the effect on including mention of SSADM in public procurement.
2. CCTA/DAB position on the relationship between ownership and control of the method, and role of BSI panel.
3. BSI view of development of the standard, particularly regarding resource and copyright issues.
4. Reappraisal of overall format of SSADM standard.
5. ERA model.

The deadline for comments on the DPC occurred after this meeting of the TP. The number of responses was not very large, but on the other hand some responses, such as that from the UG, represented a large number of interests.

The sorts of comments made fell into five main categories.

1. Questions relating to the need for a standard for SSADM.
2. The relationship between the method and the standard, including:
   (a) the need to specify mechanisms for change control and compatibility;
   (b) the conflict between the flexibility stated in Version 4, and the potential constraint of having a formal standard.
3. Format of the DPC. There were several comments on the inappropriate inclusion of topics such as 'future developments', 'IRDS', etc. There were also comments on the level of detail, and the concern that the standard should refer to the Version 4 documentation rather than repeat, paraphrase, or reinterpret it.
4. A variety of technical issues. These raised specific detailed points regarding the relationship between parts of the standard.
5. Detailed textual issues. These were for the most part requests for clarification, some of them relating to the manuals rather than to the DPC.

In the light of the comments received, and as part of the process of reaching consensus under a new convenor, and with additional members, the TP reconsidered the role of the standard itself and the likely future developments. In its meetings in the latter part of 1991 a large amount of time was devoted to consider the fundamental issues such as the need for a

Table 6.1 Responses to the Draft for Public Comment classified against each volume

Framework	ownership/control clarified change control mechanism specified references to 'current SSADM documentation' rather than to Version 4 omit all references to 'further work', future phases, other standards, etc. spell out flexibility and configuring as integral part of method
Concepts	add in mention of concepts included in 'forms'
Presentation	too detailed and too constraining some omissions, e.g. keys
Basic Products	add forms for illustrative purposes
Modules and Stages	clarify level of detail

standard, and the likely consequences of its appearance. It was concluded that, regardless of the actual EC position, there was a requirement for a clear statement of the deliverables that customers could expect from any supplier contracted for system development under the rubric of SSADM. This led to a recognition that the central focus of the standard had to be restated around the products themselves. Hence a major restructuring of the five volume DPC was demanded.

A REVISED ONE-VOLUME FORMAT

By April 1992 a revised format had been agreed. The five volume DPC was far too detailed and cumbersome. It lacked focus. Refining the purpose and focus of the standard showed that a single standard in a single volume would resolve the key issues. Work was started to produce a single volume standard, focused on the interface between customer and supplier in a contractual context. This focus would be primarily and explicitly on products, and the contractual assessment for acknowledging delivery of completed products.

The DPC 'Framework Standard' would be replaced by introductory sections detailing the role, purpose, and scope of the standard. This would stress that the structure and content of the SSADM standard would result in its being self-contained; it would not depend upon the SSADM manuals in its role as a standard. Conversely the standard would not be independent of the method (and of the manuals). The standard and the method would be developed by the BSI and the DAB, respectively, but with a clearly understood relationship to each other. This relationship would be defined in the standard, encompassing control of the method (DAB) and of the standard (BSI), as well as the change control procedures for each. Any version of the standard would always refer to a specified version of the method (manuals).

The purpose of the standard would be restated with a primary orientation on customer and supplier. Mention would also be made of the exchange or progression of products between development stages. The standard would facilitate the needs for training and tool support, but would not address these needs specifically or directly other than through product specifications.

A section on conformance would be included, addressing the role of the standard in the contractual context. This would restate BSI policy that it is not the role of any standard issued by the BSI to demand conformance. Adherence to any standard is voluntary. Customers may demand such adherence as part of their own contractual requirements; suppliers may claim conformance to the standard.

The volume of the DPC entitled 'Basic Product Descriptions' was largely a repetition of sections of the manual. The material would be replaced by a series of entries for the selected products. The products would be ordered in stages, within modules, thereby enabling users of the standard to reference products associated by stage and module. Another section of the standard would illustrate the position of products in the SSADM structure.

Each product would be clearly denoted by name, together with an indication of its status—either interim or end-stage or end-module:

- End-stage   Products that are delivered at the end of a stage, having been created or updated within that stage.
- End-module   Products which are delivered at the end of a module, having been created or updated within that module.
- Interim   Products which are created during a stage or module, but which are not specifically offered as delivered products at the end of the stage or module itself; they are often 'in-progress' products, created as part of the continuing development process, and used in the derivation of other products.

A further distinction was made between products delivered as 'completed', and those where the delivered product would be expected to be further developed in subsequent stages. For instance in SSADM Version 4 there are several forms of Data Flow Model: Current Physical, Logical, Required System. The Current Physical variant is delivered at the end of stage 1, and modified in stage 2 as a basis for the development of the Logical variant. This modification is not the result of any flaws in the model, but merely an effect of the later development activities.

These distinctions between product types would provide developers and customers with a basis on which they could decide upon their overall quality strategy, e.g. whether to assess all products, exclude interim ones, and so on.

In the detailed section of product specifications, against each product there would be details of the purpose behind the product, its composition, and the criteria to be applied to ensure satisfactory delivery of a complete product. In addition, there would be details of the graphical representation of the product, where such a form was relevant. There would be no separate 'Presentation Conventions' standard. Against any specific product, only those aspects that can be graphically presented in SSADM Version 4 will be the subject of a 'preferred format'.

The emphasis would be on illustrating the key components of the representation, rather than on offering complete examples. Although this was a stronger view of presentation than that defined in the manuals, the TP felt that the standard must offer a baseline for readability and comprehensibility across a range of contexts. To this end a 'preferred' presentation would be given. It would, however, be made clear that conformance to the standard could be achieved using alternative presentation conventions, as long as the products delivered could be shown to fulfil the completion criteria.

The material included in the 'Modelling Concepts' would be removed unless it impinged directly on the assessment of specific products. There would be no separate section on concepts themselves. This also applied to the 'Modules and Stages' standard. The discussion of the completion criteria for any product would refer to the relevant criteria for a specific stage or module if more than one was included.

There would be a single glossary, with every entry assumed to duplicate equivalent information in the manual. Any divergence from this supposition would be emphasized, and the differences noted. It was stressed that the expression of such divergences in the standard was not meant to pre-empt their eventual resolution by the DAB. The DAB had ultimate responsibility for progression of the method.

On the basis of this agreed, revised format the next development phase for the standard began. It would include a review by the UG as well as by those who had sent comments on the DPC. It involved a good deal of effort, but there was no way in which the DPC could otherwise have been transformed into a publishable standard.

One final note: the TP recommended that the ERA model be withdrawn from potential circulation by BSI. For the immediate future the model would not play any part in the standard. A copy of the model, and associated documentation, was lodged with the UG Technical Committee, and they would arrange a mechanism and timetable for responses from UG members to the CCTA concerning the possible development and eventual use of the model. To date no response has been forthcoming regarding the

ERA model, and it appears that it will be relegated to the role of historical curiosity.

Although at first glance there seemed to be a significant difference between the five volume DPC and the single volume draft envisaged, this was not in fact the case. The revised version had been explicitly derived from the DPC in the light of the substantive responses received. It was technically and functionally equivalent to the DPC. It was important to stress this, otherwise the TP would have had to publish a further DPC, with a similar three-month period for comment, followed by a review procedure.

COMPLETING AND PUBLISHING THE STANDARD

By mid-1992 the main work on the revised document had been completed. The revised document was sent to all members of the TP, even those who had not attended frequently. By early 1993 the TP called a meeting to decide that the text was in a state ready for publication, and that it should be presented to the BSI and IST/15 for approval and eventual publication.

The text now consisted of the following:

1. An introductory section, including a list of definitions of terms used.
2. Details of the specifications of the products themselves—grouped in conceptual categories.
3. Diagrams explaining the links between products.
4. Diagrams locating products in the relevant modules.
5. Alphabetic listing of products cross-referenced to the relevant section of the detailed specifications.

The manuscript had been sent directly to a BSI editor. This proved enormously useful, as many of the points raised from this led to clarification of the text. This revised text was then presented to the parent committee (IST/15) who have to give approval. This proved to be a useful review procedure since those commenting had some technical expertise, but also were distanced from the development process, and so raised issues of clarification that those on the TP had come to assume were self-evident.

By mid-1993 all the various procedures had been completed, and the final editing stages were started. Unfortunately these proved lengthy, and it was only in June 1994 that the standard finally appeared.

Following the various editorial procedures the overall shape of the standard had altered slightly. It consists of an introductory section, including a Foreword explaining the background to the standard, its relationship to the method, and the change control procedure; there is also an Introduction, outlining the structure of SSADM. There is a section describing the scope of the standard, and a listing of the definitions of terms used. This list has 239 entries, taken predominantly from the Version 4 manuals.

The main body of the text consists of the detailed specifications of each of the application products. The products are grouped into conceptual headings as follows:

Business Systems Option Products
Data Flow Modelling Products
Dialogue Design Products
Entity–Event Modelling Products
Function Definition Products
Logical Data Modelling Products
Logical Database Process Design Products
Process Specification Products
Relational Data Analysis Products
Requirements Definition Products
Specification Prototyping Products
Technical Systems Options Products
Physical Data Design Products
Physical Process Specification Products
Physical Environment Description Products
Miscellaneous Products

A brief description of each heading is given prior to the details for the relevant products in that group. Each individual product specification included in the standard is then presented in the following format (the details of the product entries are taken from BS 7738: 1994):

Name of product

1 *Purpose:* To permit full and accurate specification of a type of product. This specifies the purpose of the product or component. For clarity this may be expressed in terms of the objectives for using the product.

2 *Composition:* There are two different approaches to this element depending on the product involved: composition by component (showing the component structure of a product); and composition by product breakdown (showing that a specified product consists of a hierarchically organized set of components, each of which is itself a product). For some of these hierarchies a product breakdown diagram is included as a reference.

3 *Completion criteria:* These will indicate features of the product that can be assessed to determine its adequacy and integrity. These criteria may invoke adherence to a specific notation (syntax), as well as to the relevance and meaning of the product to the specific project context (semantics). It is likely that many of these criteria can only be assessed by users' representatives in conjunction with other project personnel. In addition, many of the products are of importance in the later development stages of the information system, and must therefore be readily available and identifiable by the relevant members of the development team. Furthermore, if products require revision and reworking, suitable configuration principles need to be established to ensure that team members are working from the same variants of products. Establishing a satisfactory and effective review and quality strategy, and configuration regime, are not addressed specifically in the standard. It is suggested that reference be made to the relevant standards on quality and configuration management.

In the category of miscellaneous products, some entries refer to non-SSADM products. In these instances the heading of 'completion criteria' has been amended to 'acceptance criteria', i.e. relating to the criteria for accepting the product as an input to the SSADM project.

Note: There are occasions when information or resources outside of the SSADM project are required for completion of particular tasks, and thus products. These could be a possible source of problems and delays that could affect the project but are outside the direct control of the SSADM project itself. Since in many cases these issues are generally applicable rather than product specific, they have not been included in the completion criteria. They may have to be considered as part of the overall project review and quality strategy, with appropriate contingency plans and strategies prepared in advance.

4   *Status:* This states whether the product is an end-stage, end-module or interim product; also whether it is delivered completed in the first instance, or evolves during further stages.

A further distinction is made between end-stage/end-module products that are delivered as complete at the end of the stage or module, and those that are delivered but expected to evolve or be the subject of further refinement in later stages or modules.

5   *Presentation:* This gives details of the presentation conventions to be used for graphical components of the product. It is only applicable to products with non-textual components.

Commentary and recommendations on the above

This starts with an introduction comprising a brief description of the product. It also includes any general background information.

- *Derivation*   This identifies the products that are used in the development of the product. In some cases the derivation may involve earlier versions of the product itself, particularly with evolving products.
- *Where used*   A list indicating the stage and/or module in which the particular product is used in the method. Entries may also indicate the specific technique with which it will be associated.

MAKING THE STANDARD USABLE

In order to enhance the usability of the standard, various appendices are included to assist those looking for specific products or groups of related products. Thus there is a series of product grouping diagrams (e.g. Fig. 6.1 showing the grouping for stage 5) showing the products normally associated with a specific stage or module. There is also a series of conformity charts (e.g. Fig. 6.2) 'listing products by the stage or module in which they might be expected to be created or updated' (BS7738, p. 125). The idea is that relevant charts are completed by contractual parties clarifying the expectations of both supplier and client.

In general the first responses to the standard have been most encouraging. Even those closely involved in the development of the standard have expressed themselves pleasantly surprized at the 'look and feel' of the finished product. Only time will tell, however, if BS7738: 1994 is truly fit for its purpose.

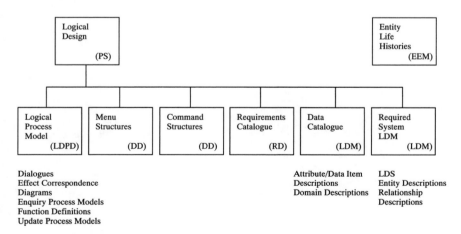

Figure 6.1 BS7738 product groupings for stage 5.

Product name	Reference	Status (1, 2, 3)	Conformity (A, B)	Presentation convention (Y/N)
Cost/Benefit Analysis	3.1.3	1[1]		
Data Catalogue (see table D.8)	3.6.2	2		
Data Flow Model (see table D.9)	3.2.4	see 3.2.4.4		
Feasibility Report	3.1.5	1		
Impact Analysis	3.1.6	1[1]		
Logical Data Model (see table D.10)	3.6.5	2		
Non-selected Feasibility Option(s)	3.1.4	3		
Requirements Catalogue	3.10.1	see 3.10.1.4		
Selected Feasibility Option	3.1.4	1		
User Catalogue	3.10.4	3		

[1]Delivered complete for selected option; interim product for non-selected option(s)

Figure 6.2 BS7738 conformity chart for feasibility Module, Stage 0: Feasibility

7

CONCLUSION

In the preceding chapters I have sought to outline the role that standards can play in the IS domain; and the issues that arise around the activity of standardization itself. This then prepared the ground for a detailed analysis of the development of the standard for SSADM.

In presenting this material, the idea has been to outline some of the main principles behind standards themselves, and to answer a number of questions that arise whenever the topic of standards is considered—and to do so explicitly with regard to IS standards and standardization.

Some of the questions asked are listed in Table 7.1, together with the chapter(s) that deal with the answers.

What I have also sought to explain is that the IS domain is fraught with complexities that make standardization both difficult and essential. These issues are not simply or even predominantly technical, but emanate from the sorts of market pressures outlined by authors such as Cargill, Gabel, and Gray. In addition, the IS domain is more than one of products and purchases. Issues such as service provision, standardized procedures, and future planning affect the situation, and complicate any simple market-based argument. Other standards issues such as those for quality are also influential.

This is not to deny that one useful test for a standard being truly required is that it should be possible to envisage a subeconomy developing around its enforcement, implementation, certification, etc. This is essentially arguing that for a standard to operate effectively there must be people willing to resource its enforcement and certification—a net benefit: a useful test against which many current standards developments should be assessed.

The development of the standard for SSADM was financed by the CCTA. Whether there will be support for the full operation, enforcement, and updating of the standard in future remains to be seen.

This *market testing* is a better test than any abstract idea of perfection. As Cargill notes, 'Perfect standards are no longer the goal; instead, the focus is on obtaining a workable and acceptable standard within a time frame that will allow it to be useful' (1989, p. 41).

However, the impact and relevance of standards cannot be fully appreciated without consideration of the overall and organizational contexts within which the standards are meant to operate. These concerns were discussed under the rubric of 'maturity', and the main point of the discussion was to indicate that organizational preparedness and learning has to be taken into account—including cultural, collective, and individual aspects of competence and experience.

The development of the standard for SSADM illustrates that workability and acceptability do not occur automatically in standards making, and that there are many obstacles and problems in seeking to develop standards in these less tangible areas of IS. Only time will tell if the decisions taken with regard to the standard were correct. On the other hand, if organizations experience problems in implementing the standard, it may be the fault of the standard itself; but it could also be caused by the 'technological immaturity' of the organization in question.

Table 7.1

What are standards, exactly?	BS0 definition given in Chapter 1; Appendix outlines distinctions between *de jure* and *de facto* standards
How are they devised and defined?	Chapter 1 discusses the process of standardization in principle Chapter 2 looks at the problems of standardization in the IS/SE domain Chapters 5 and 6 give a blow-by-blow account of the development of the SSADM standard
Why are they needed?	Chapters 1 and 2 attempt various explanations for this, using the work of Cargill and Gabel, among others
How do standards in the IS realm differ from those in other areas?	Chapter 2 deals explicitly with this point
How long do they take to develop?	Chapters 5 and 6 give an example, but not necessarily a representative one. All that can be said is that like most complex projects, standards take longer to develop than initially scheduled!
How much do they cost to develop, enforce, and maintain?	This is an issue far too complex to afford simple responses. Gabel's ideas about the role of the market, and the cost/benefit balances are an indication of the sorts of complexities involved
What is the relationship between standards and legal obligations, particularly those contained in contractual documents?	The simple answer is that a 'British Standard does not purport to include all the necessary provisions of a contract' (BSI, on back cover of all their current standards). Chapter 6 indicates some of the wider issues
How does a person, group or organization contribute to standards making?	Chapters 1 and 2 discuss this, and Cargill (1989) offers further advice
How are standards limited by national frontiers?	Chapters 1, 2 and 6 cover some of this aspect
How do standards interact?	Although not covered specifically, Chapters 2–4 go some way in dealing with this, but the specific relationships between groups of standards are far too complex for the present discussion
Who regulates them in operation, and adjudicates between disputants or litigants?	This issue is not covered. It will, however, be interesting to chart the use and responses to the BS for SSADM as a case study in this area
How and when can standards be applied?	Chapter 3 deals with this specifically for the IS domain

APPENDIX

A NOTE ON *DE FACTO* STANDARDS

De jure standards are those that are officially sanctioned by an appropriate certification body such as the BSI or the ISO. *De facto* standards, on the other hand, are usually defined simply as unofficial standards. Partly as a response to the growth of *de facto* standards in areas such as IS/IT, JTC1* has now recognized the role of such unofficial standards, and that they may form components or be associated with official ones. This, however, requires a more positive definition of *de facto* standards. An early attempt to produce such a definition has been forthcoming from a group within BSI and it is worth quoting from their draft document as follows:

> . . . there is a spectrum of standards. This includes:
> — . . . ISO/IEC standards . . .
> —other specifications which are the result of varying degrees of international consensus and are owned by organizations which may or may not be willing to co-operate with JTC1 committees
> — . . . proprietary specifications which are owned by, and restricted to, single companies

---

*JTC1 is the joint committee combining both the International Standards Organization (ISO) and the International Electrotechnical Commission (IEC). Several international standards making fora such as that for Software Engineering (SC7) come under the auspices of JTC1.

. . . factors [which] need to be considered . . .
availability of a specification . . .
    —is there a complete, accurate and stable document?
    —is it independent of any other, non-standard technology?
    —does it conform to JTC1 requirements for standards?
    —is it publicly available?
. . . process by which the specification is developed and maintained . . .
    —to what extent did the specification result from an open international consensus process?
    —is the owning organization willing to contribute to the work of standardization and subsequent maintenance?
    —is the specification owned by a single-interest organization or by a consortium with wide representation?
. . . stability of the specification
    —is the specification implemented by products which have proved to meet the needs of users?

This may help bodies such as JTC1 in their need to reference and incorporate *de facto* standards, but even if the answer to all of the above questions was 'no', a specification could still act as a *de facto* standard if it fulfilled the criteria mentioned in Chapter 1 sufficiently widely.

REFERENCES

Aujla, S., Bryant, A. and Semmens, L. (1994), 'Applying formal methods within structured development', *IEEE Journal on Selected Areas in Communications*, 12(2).

Boaden, R. and Lockett, G. (1991), 'Information technology, information systems and information management', *European Journal of Information Systems*, 1(1).

Boehm, B. (1986), 'A spiral model of software development and enhancement', *ACMSIGSOFT*, Vol. II, August, pp. 14–24.

Boehm, B., *et al.* (1978), *Characteristics of Software Quality*, North Holland, Amsterdam.

Brooks, F. P. (1986), 'No silver bullet', in H.-J. Kugler (ed.), *Information Processing '86*, North-Holland, Amsterdam.

Bryant, A. (1989), 'Better professionals for the tools', in G. X. Ritter (ed.) *Information Processing '89, Proceedings of the 11th IFIP World Computer Congress*, North-Holland, Amsterdam.

Bryant, A. (1991), 'The myth of the information society', in J. Berleur and J. Drumm (eds), *Information Technology Assessment, Proceedings of the 4th IFIP Conference on Human Choice and Computers*, North-Holland, Amsterdam.

Bryant, A. and Grogan, J. (1993), 'Developments in quality in information systems development', in *Proceedings of the Conference on Software Quality Assurance (SQA93)*.

Bryant, A. and Evans, A. (1994), 'OO oversold: obscure objects of desire', *Information & Software Technology*, 36(1).

BS0: 1991 A Standard for Standards; in 3 parts, 3rd edn, British Standards Institution.

Cargill, C. F. (1989), *Information Technology Standardization: Theory, Process and Organizations*, Digital Press.

Charette, R. (1992), 'Gaining value from your IT supplier', *Software Management*, 34(summer).

Constantine, L. L. and Yourdon. E. (1979), *Structured Design*, Prentice-Hall.

Crosby, P. B. (1979), *Quality is Free*, McGraw-Hill, New York.

Deming, W. E. (1982), *Quality, Productivity and Competitive Advantage*, MIT Center for Advanced Engineering Study.

Dreyfus, H. L. and Dreyfus S. E., *Mind over Machine*, Blackwell, Oxford.

Gabel, H. L. (1991), *Competitive Strategies for Product Standards*, McGraw-Hill, New York.

Gray, P. (1991), *Open Systems: A Business Strategy for the 1990s*, McGraw-Hill, New York.

Heym, M. and Osterle, H. (1991), *A Reference Model of Information Systems Development*, Version 1.2.

Humphrey, W. S. (1989), *Managing the Software Process*, Addison-Wesley, Reading, Mass.

IEEE (1993) *Master Plan for Software Engineering Standards*, Version 0.6.

ImproveIT (1991), Issue 1.0, June, Admiral PLC, Cranfield Institute of Technology and Ministry of Defence.

ISO 8402 (1986) *Quality Vocabulary*, ISO.

Jackson, I. (1986), *Corporate Information Management*, Prentice-Hall, Englewood Cliffs, NJ.

JTCI (1992) 'Information technology—standardization framework for software engineering', editor's draft, Version 2.0.

Logica (1988) Logica for DTI, *Quality Management Standards for Software*, Department of Trade and Industry.

Longley, D. L. and Shain, M. (1985), *Macmillan Dictionary of Information Technology*, 2nd edn, Macmillan, London.

Lyytinen, K. (1987), 'A taxonomic perspective of IS development', in R. J. Boland and R. A. Hirschheim (eds), *Critical Issues in IS Research*, Wiley, New York.

Marciniak, J. and Reifer, D. (1990), *Software Acquisition Management*, Wiley, New York.

McCall, J. (1979), 'An introduction to software quality metrics', in J. Cooper and M. Fisher (eds), *Software Quality Management*, Petrocelli, New York.

Nolan, R. (1982), *Managing the Data Resource*, 2nd edn, West.

Ould, M. and Miller, C. (1992), 'The evolution of quality standards: ISO 9001, TickIT, ImproveIT and Quantum', *Software Quality Management*, 15(summer).

Pressman, R. (1992), *Software Engineering: A Practitioner's Approach*, 3rd edn, McGraw-Hill, New York.

Price Waterhouse (1988) Price Waterhouse for DTI, *Software Quality Standards: The Costs and Benefits*, Department of Trade and Industry.

Quantum (1992) *The Quantum Study Report*.

Schach, S. (1993), *Software Engineering*, 2nd edn, Aksen Associates and Irwin Inc.

Simon, H. (1983), *The Sciences of the Artificial*, MIT.

Slater, J. A. (1991), 'The TickIT certfication scheme', *Colloquium on TickIT Certification Initiatives: Objectives and Practice*, IEE.

SMARTIE (1992) Standards and Methods Assessment using Rigorous Techniques in Industrial Environments—Report on Measurable Standards Attributes, CSSR, City University.

Sommerville, I. (1992), *Software Engineering*, 4th edn, Addison Wesley.

SSADM (1985) *SSADM Version 2 Training Manual*, Issue 1.

SSADM (1986) *SSADM Version 3 Reference Manual*, Issue 1, 4 vols CCTA; later republished in 2 vols by Blackwell (1987).

SSADM (1990) *SSADM Version 4 Reference Manual*, NCC/Blackwell.

TickIT (1992) Department of Trade and Industry, *TickIT Making a Better Job of Software: A Guide to Software QMS Construction and Certification using ISO 9001/EN 29001/BS 5750 Part 1*, Issue 2.0.

Wernham, B. (1991), 'Is PRINCE a quality management system?', *Software Quality Management*, 11 August.

INDEX

Further titles in this Series

Related titles are available in McGraw-Hill's International Software Quality Assurance Series